Touched by Suicide

Touched by Suicide

A Personal and Psychological Perspective on the Longing for Death and Rebirth

Christi Taylor-Jones
MA, MFT, Certified Jungian Analyst

CHIRON PUBLICATIONS • ASHEVILLE, NORTH CAROLINA

© 2024 by Chiron Publications. All rights reserved. No part of this publication may be reproduced, stored in a retrieval system, or transmitted, in any form by any means, electronic, mechanical, photocopying, recording, or otherwise, without the prior written permission of the publisher, Chiron Publications, P.O. Box 19690, Asheville, N.C. 28815-1690.

www.ChironPublications.com

Interior and cover design by Danijela Mijailovic
Printed primarily in the United States of America.

ISBN 978-1-68503-506-8 paperback
ISBN 978-1-68503-507-5 hardcover
ISBN 978-1-68503-510-5 electronic
ISBN 978-1-68503-508-2 limited edition paperback
ISBN 978-1-68503-509-9 limited edition hardcover

Library of Congress Cataloging-in-Publication Data Pending

To my analyst,

whose commitment to my healing and individuation process changed the course of my life, and taught me how to transform meaningless suffering into meaningful suffering.

If we want to move toward self-knowledge and the experience of reality, then an enquiry into suicide becomes the first step.
—James Hillman

CONTENTS

Preface	1
Acknowledgments	5
Introduction	7
1. Suicide Up Close and Personal	11
2. The Who, How, and Why of Suicide: An Overview	47
3. Historical Attitudes Toward Suicide	53
4. Suicide and the Soul	65
5. Jung and Suicide	71
6. Modern Views of Suicide	81
7. Suicide and Shame	99
8. Suicide and Depression	127
9. Suicide and Trauma	143
10. Transformation: An Unconscious Human Longing	159
11. A Clinical Perspective: Two Cases of Suicide	167
12. Summary and Reflections	187

Appendix 1: The Case of Suicide in Seattle	199
Appendix 2: Statistical Overview of Suicide Rates Worldwide and in the United States	201
Appendix 3: Neurobiological and Genetic Factors in Suicide	221
Notes	225
Bibliography	239
About the Author	265

PREFACE

My brother's suicide in 2015 served as an impetus for me to write this book. Prior to my brother's death, I experienced several other suicidal impulses—both in my personal life, and in my professional life as a Jungian analyst. These included an attempted suicide of my own, a suicidal gesture by my mother, and the suicides of a close family friend and of my father-in-law, as well as my ex-husband buying and putting a gun to his head. I'd also heard about numerous suicides undertaken by well-known people, and little known, or even unknown people, whose names appeared in the news. I began to feel as if suicide was an everyday occurrence. Had it always been this way, or did the prevalence of suicide have something to do with the times in which we lived?

At one time, I believed suicide to be a consequence of severe mental illness. I included myself in that category. What else could explain such a desperate and selfish act? Yet, over the years, I heard clients of mine talk about wanting to kill themselves, most of whom I did not consider mentally ill. Certainly, I did not consider them *severely* mentally ill, and my own analyst agreed that it was not mental illness that had prompted my own suicide attempt. Being in analysis helped me understand the combined circumstances that made me want to end my life. In this book, I will explain what prompted my attempt, and what has led many others down this path.

The very existence of suicide reflects the inherent tension in all of us between the will to live and the desire to die. On the one hand, we will do anything to survive. But, when life is bereft of meaning and joy, we may want to escape. We experience fleeting thoughts of wishing we were dead to avoid enduring our current circumstances. Most of the time, these thoughts are outweighed by the will to live, so we muddle through until we feel better. We may even vacillate for an entire lifetime between longing to live and wanting to die, caught between the two, not fully living, but not choosing to die. We don't tell anyone about it. If, however, our painful life experiences and dark feelings become chronic, we may actively, rather than passively, seek an exit, one that will take us out of a hopeless life. At this point, thinking about dying turns to planning our death. This is when suicide becomes a real possibility, and not just a fleeting thought. The plan may be impulsive, or years in the making. We may eventually carry it out. If we succeed, life as we know it ends. If not, we have another chance at life. We also have another chance at a successful suicide plan.

My guess is that, if you opened this book, you fall into one of the following categories: either you know someone who has committed or contemplated suicide, or you have tried it yourself, or you have thought about it. If so, you may be seeking to better understand your own motives, or those of someone else. You may also be wanting to quell your own shame, fear, or grief about it. If you are a mental-health professional or researcher, you might be interested in learning about a more depth-oriented approach to the subject in order to further your own research, or to help suicidal clients in your practice. In each case, the aim of this book is to add to your understanding.

As a psychotherapist and analyst practicing the depth psychology of C. G. Jung, I am on the frontlines of people's desire to die, as well as to live. I sit with them in their ambivalence and help them explore the roots of their desire to stop living. I know this place in the human psyche because I have experienced it in myself. I don't judge it, and while I am invested in their continuing to live, I respect their desire to die. Sometimes transformation is possible, and sometimes it's not. Sometimes a client's desire to die becomes a *will* to die. All I can do is hope that they have seriously considered both life and death, and the consequences of choosing each. I have watched people wrestle with this choice, sometimes for years, sometimes only briefly. To share what I have learned from being on the battlefield of life and death is the reason I have written this book.

ACKNOWLEDGMENTS

No published work is created by a single individual. This one is no exception. I had much support and help in transforming an idea into an article that eventually became a book. I first introduced the idea of writing a book on suicide to my Jungian writing group, which gave me the confidence to pursue it. After that, friends and colleagues, such as Jungian analyst Janis Jennings, offered early and astute editorial suggestions that set me on the right track, as well as gave me unending emotional support throughout. Numerous other colleagues shared their own stories of suicide and offered advice, both legal and literary, that added richness to the content.

My computer genius, Kevin, helped me with technological problems, and Christophe Le Mouel, executive director of the Los Angeles Jung Institute, assisted me in figuring out the editing program I needed to use. Christophe also helped usher my article, "When Shame Becomes Deadly: The Relationship between Suicidality and Shame; A Personal Perspective," through its publication in *Psychological Perspectives* in the fall of 2023.

However, I would not have a polished manuscript were it not for my devoted editor, Sharron Dorr, whose tireless attention to detail, accuracy, and clarity challenged me at every turn. Sharron continuously forced me to think, and rethink, about what I was writing, and why. I thank analyst and author, Michael Gellert, for referring me to Sharron. Michael also supported me through the publishing process, offering his good advice. I also owe a debt to my editor at Chiron who added the finishing touches and made sure all the T's were crossed and the I's dotted.

Most of all, I thank the clients, whose stories inspired me to write a story about suicide—from the inside. Some of their stories have been included in the text. Finally, I want to thank my son, who has always urged me to continue writing, and to whom, in his capacity as a doctor, I turned to for help in translating studies about the brain into laymen's language.

INTRODUCTION

This book is not just about committing suicide; it is also about attempting it, or even merely *thinking* about it. It's about the delicate balance with which many of us struggle. In fact, few people make it through life with no thought whatsoever of wanting to be dead, even if that desire is more symbolic than concrete.

If you are reading this book, you likely know someone who has committed suicide, or have entertained the idea yourself. The reality is, most people can name at least one person that they have known, who has died from suicide. It is estimated that eight hundred thousand people around the world die of suicide each year.[1] That number has increased 60 percent in the last forty-five years.[2] *Suicide is now the tenth leading cause of death in the United States, and that rate is even higher among certain segments of society.*[3]

Despite its prevalence, suicide remains shrouded in shame, fear, and grief, which explains why no one wants to talk about it. Unfortunately, silence just adds to the mystery and misery. In his book, *Why People Die by Suicide*, Thomas Joiner recounts the reactions of various people in his life to his father's suicide. He said, "No one understood it, really." Either they got "tripped up by intellectual understanding," or they "ignored it altogether.. . . . So great is the taboo on suicide that some people will not say a word."[4]

According to Clancy Martin, who wrote about the death of celebrity chef and television host, Anthony Bourdain, for every person who dies by suicide, about 280 people are considering it.[5] He notes that "suicide, for most people, is a process."[6] Suicidal ideation can begin at a very young age. Some people make several attempts and survive all of them, while others, such as Anthony Bourdain, make only one and die from it. Others think about it constantly but never make the attempt. Says Martin, "Humans are complicated, contradictory creatures, full of irrationality and cognitive and emotional dissonance. We are allowed to be both grateful for life and desperate to escape it."[7]

There are many reasons why people end their life, and in this book, I will describe them to you. However, the through line for me, and for many people, is a powerful longing for transformation and rebirth. Suicide may seem the only option when life as one knows it has become untenable in some way that cannot be controlled or escaped from—or at least the person *thinks* it can't.

I will point out some commonalities among those who kill themselves, and I will discuss risk factors based on personal and sociological traits, age, economics, race, neurobiology, family history, and cultural values. Another factor may be the time in which we live. The pull toward death may lessen at certain times in history and ramp up at other times. The Great Depression, and periods of national or world upheaval, are times when suicide rates have increased. I do believe that we are now living in a

Introduction

time when psychological and sociological energies are aligned in favor of self-destruction, bombarded as our human culture is by mass murders, terrorism, polarization, war, and the threat of environmental annihilation. These factors, to name a few, make it imperative that we understand the phenomenon of suicide in all its forms.

I have attempted here to weave together personal and clinical experience with research on the social, psychological, historical, and religious aspects of suicide. My study of the subject ranged from the attitudes toward suicide in ancient Greece and world religions to our modern approach to suicide. After much research, what I came to, or came back to, was my own story, which I realized was a human story, an archetypal story. I wanted to write about suicide from the vantage point of someone who had experienced it from the *inside*—and had lived to talk about it.

One falsehood I would like to dispel is that killing oneself is always an irrational act, the result of mental illness or weakness of character. It is true that a common denominator in most cases is unbearable suffering. However, some suicides can be described as altruistic, heroic, or even necessary to the survival of the species or tribe. In that way, suicide is no different in humans than it is among creatures in the animal kingdom. We know, for example, that certain insects will sacrifice themselves for the good of the colony, and that others will stop eating when in grief. Birds in stress have been known to pull out their feathers, even denuding themselves before pecking at their flesh. Accounts of animals in captivity killing themselves is not unknown. For example, after twelve years of performing for people, an orca whale fatally slammed himself against a wall after exhibiting signs of distress.[8]

Another myth is that suicide is the direct result of depression. While depression may be one of many factors, it is not the only one, and it is the easiest to treat. Equating suicide with depression dismisses the importance of other forms of suicide, including assisted suicides, which are the result of conscious, considered decision making. Inherent in the term *assisted suicide* is the assumption of support. Such suicides are not carried out alone, in secret, or in shame. The ill and suffering person chooses to die a peaceful death with dignity. Some argue that the same should apply to those suffering from severe psychological distress. I discuss the pros and cons of this idea in the book.

Regardless of what else may be going on in the life of a suicidal person, the desire for rebirth is often an unconscious motivating factor. Consciously, the suicidal individual wants to end their torment, but underneath that is a longing for some kind of change or transformation. In my experience, suicidality almost always signals a need for something to die, but what needs to die may not be the physical person. The challenge is to discover the meaning in one's suffering. If one cannot find it, he or she may end the suffering by any means possible, including suicide. Doing so, however, denies suffering its value. My hope is that in reading this book, you will consider the meaning in your own suffering, as well as in the suffering of others. As a result, you may have more compassion and empathy for those driven to suicide.

1

SUICIDE UP CLOSE AND PERSONAL

We never come fully to grips with life until we are willing to wrestle with death. . . .
And the problem of death is posed most vividly in suicide.

—James Hillman

My personal experience with suicide is dominated by the tragedy of my own brother's death. Here, I will include what led up to it, what may have motivated it, and how it impacted me as a survivor. Most notably, his death inspired me to learn, research, and write about the subject, first for myself, and later for a larger audience. My brother was the most recent victim of suicide in my family, but I had previously experienced my mother's suicidal gesture, my own failed attempt, the suicide of a close family friend, and the death of my father-in-law before realizing how much I'd been touched by the impulse to self-destruct.

As a therapist, I have also encountered suicidal clients, including one who took his life shortly after ending therapy with me. Slowly, I've begun to realize how many people think about killing themselves, even if they don't act on it. The next chapter details the numbers of people in various categories who commit or attempt suicide. These are just numbers, however. They don't tell the individual stories. My intent in revealing my brother's story, and my own, is to put a face to suicide and provide a context in which to view the statistics. I will call him Jimmy, although that was not his real name.

My Brother's Story

It was a warm October morning. The shrimp and clams were still on ice, awaiting their simmering encounter in a delicious cioppino stew. Bottles of red wine and loaves of French bread with garlic butter, were set on the counter. Despite the excitement of being joined by several friends for a birthday party, I felt a strange sense of dread that I could not put my finger on. I pulled the lettuce, tomato, cucumber, and other salad ingredients from the refrigerator. I would make the salad first, and let it chill while I started the cioppino.

That's when the phone rang. I hoped it wasn't someone canceling at the last minute. Instead, I heard the voice of my father's dear friend and neighbor. She seemed worried and expressed concern that she hadn't seen anyone enter or leave my father's house for several days, even to collect the newspaper. That was unusual. She had tried to reach my father by phone, but there was no answer. Something was wrong. She was afraid to knock on the door for fear Jimmy might answer. He had recently banned the neighbor from my father's house, despite my father's protests. My brother didn't like this woman. She was one of an increasing number of people he disliked, and because my mother had died several years before, my brother was serving as my father's caretaker. This gave him a certain amount of control over my father, who was ninety-two.

At one time, Jimmy had been a successful physical therapist. He was married, had a son, and was well respected in the community. But he had a darker side to him. He carried a great deal of anger, which he tried to medicate with alcohol. Although he was never diagnosed, he suffered from ADHD and had struggled in school as a child. Nevertheless, he managed to graduate from college and go on to graduate school. His humor buffered some of his anger, but even that could turn dark, carrying offensive undertones.

He tended to hold grudges, mostly against family members, including my uncle and cousin, and even my father and me. He was incapable of communicating his anger—or indeed, *any* feelings directly, and expressed them in passive-aggressive ways instead. He held onto even minor infractions, including the one by the neighbor. At the time, she had promised to take my father to the doctor, but at the last minute had been unable to do so due to family issues of her own.

Jimmy's resentments were long standing, including grudges against me. He never forgave me, for example, for organizing a family intervention meant to encourage him to enter treatment for his alcoholism. He also never forgave me for lamenting in a letter to him that, even though we had never been close, I longed for a real sister-brother relationship. I wrote it while he was in treatment, hoping that once he was sober, we could become closer. We didn't share much in common, even as children. He was into sports, while my sister and I enjoyed the arts. Also, I was a good student, while he struggled academically. Our one area of agreement was politics, but even so, during our discussions, he felt a need to depart from me.

As a child, I found Jimmy annoying, the way big sisters often do. My younger sister was born ten years after Jimmy, and I think he had hoped for a brother. I, on the other hand, was delighted to have a sister and was always very close to her. After I moved out and went to college, Jimmy bullied her. I think he resented our close relationship, and, even after I left home, they were never close.

Jimmy was also disappointed that he failed to make the basketball team, which would have made my father proud. Both of my parents were athletic. That's the one characteristic he did share with them over the years. He had hoped to grow to a height that would allow him to be a star, as my father had been. But, while my father was six foot three, my brother stopped growing at five foot ten—not tall enough for major teams. My father was also more agile on the court and had had the makings of a real athlete. In high school he made "all-city" in Los Angeles. He remained tall and slender throughout life, while my brother had gained weight after he married, and remained overweight thereafter. At times, he tried to get in shape through exercise, but the alcohol interfered.

Jimmy never left the small town he grew up in, except to go away to college. I, on the other hand, moved a lot. Our lives couldn't have been more different, except that we had both had a son, also three years apart. When we both became parents in our thirties, it was the one commonality I thought would bring us closer, but it didn't. He wasn't one to talk about his feelings, but then no one in the family did. We nevertheless got together for family gatherings, especially when our sons were young.

In his fifties, Jimmy got a DUI. Shortly afterward, his wife divorced him, not just because of his drinking, but also because of his verbal abuse and disagreements with her about how to raise their son. Once she left, he was without a job, or the ability to drive, having lost both his driver's license, and his license to practice physical therapy. By the time he moved in with my father a few years later, he was broke, homeless, and living in a dried-up riverbed a short distance away. Whatever shame he carried from childhood—that deep sense of unworthiness stemming from failed attempts to gain parental and social acceptance—got magnified by these events. He covered it up with anger and negative projections onto other people. Both his anger, and his drinking alcohol escalated, especially after my mother's death when he was in his late forties.

My father reluctantly took him in, but soon discovered how abusive he could be when he drank alcohol. This pattern of drinking alcohol and verbal abuse increased over the years. It had been evident even when my mother was alive, but neither of my parents were able to set boundaries around Jimmy's behavior. My mother's own father had been an alcoholic, and she had loved him dearly, often blaming my grandmother for his unhappiness. She made similar excuses for my brother. After her death, my brother seemed to slowly sink into an even darker place. His drinking and his depression intensified.

Eventually, my father requested that he leave. Jimmy resisted. When things became untenable, I suggested my father get a restraining order, which he did; but as his own health diminished due to the stress, he resigned himself to housing my brother in return for the assistance he needed. I felt the underlying animosity between them whenever I visited. My father seemed annoyed that my brother could not restrain himself from making nasty remarks to upset everyone. Dad would often say, "Can't we just get along with each other and have a nice visit?!" My sister and I knew that wasn't possible. Occasionally, I would say something back to my brother, at which point my father would become exasperated, unable to control the tension in the family.

After a few years of this behavior, my brother bought a gun and threatened to kill himself. I encouraged my father to call the police, who removed the gun they found in the garage. After that, the family organized an intervention, facilitated by a local therapist. Jimmy's son and ex-wife, my sister, my husband, son, and myself all attended. Unfortunately, the ordeal only served to further inflame Jimmy. Months later, the police returned his gun to him. I don't know what happened to it, but later I tried to enroll him in a detox program, imploring the attendants at the facility to place him on a forty-eight-hour hold for his own protection. Because he denied any suicidality, they had no legal authority to hold him. If he denied being suicidal, there was nothing anyone could do. In the United States, the ability to have someone involuntarily committed to a hospital—other than by a mental health professional—ended during the former President Ronald Reagan administration. As it now stands, when an individual presents as a danger to themselves, in most cases, only the suicidal person can seek help. No one can be forced to get help. My father had failed to convince Jimmy to enter a detox program, and Jimmy continued to drink once he got out.

The red flags were waving furiously after my brother's suicide threat, but everyone believed he was just gesturing to get attention, as my mother had done years earlier on Mother's Day, when she took a razor to her wrist. We were teenagers then. She only scratched the surface of the skin, but it scared us all. We figured that my brother was doing the same thing. Our fear was not that he would hurt himself, but that he might hurt someone else—maybe my father or his neighbor. Many suicides are spurred on by anger, not just depression. People express their pain in different ways.

That brings me to why I understood the neighbor's reluctance to knock on my father's door. She had told me months earlier that my brother would ride his bike in circles around her driveway in a menacing way. She felt he was doing it on purpose to frighten her. There was something demonic in the way he looked at her, she told me. She stopped visiting my dad as a result, but they continued to meet for lunch on occasion, out of sight of my brother.

When she called the day of the birthday party, she was worried sick, afraid that something terrible had happened; she needed me to intervene. I told her I'd pack my bags and drive up that day. It was a three-hour drive. I called my sister, who lived fifteen minutes from my house, and she asked to join me.

While enroute, the neighbor called again, this time with unexpected news. "Your brother is dead," she blurted into my cell phone.

Her words came as a shock, despite the foreboding feelings I had experienced from the moment she summoned me.

"Your dad was shut in the bedroom," she said. "They've taken him to the hospital."

She and another neighbor had gone to my father's house. When no one had answered the door, which was unlocked, they entered and found the two of them. My father was in his room, where he'd been for three days, without food or water, calling out to my brother. He had fallen and couldn't reach the door without his cane. The two women immediately summoned an ambulance. They found Jimmy dead in his bedroom; his face pressed into a pillow on the floor. They assumed he must have died of a heart attack.

My own heart sunk into my stomach. I relayed the news to my sister, who sensed from my demeanor that something catastrophic had happened. She gasped and covered her face. Neither of us could believe it. The words, "Your brother is dead," felt surreal.

I didn't know then that he had died by suicide. The fact that he was dead failed to register. During the rest of the trip, neither of us knew what to think, or feel, or say. So many emotions were swirling around for both of us. I felt sick. Dead? How could that be?! I admitted that at times I had wished he would die so that my father would not be burdened by his constant anger. But did I really wish that he were dead, or merely that his abusive and destructive behavior would cease? *Dead* sounded so final. I felt guilty for my wishful thinking. Reassuring me, my sister said that she'd had similar thoughts, but neither of us could conceive of him as being actually *dead*. He was only sixty-three.

When we arrived in town, we drove directly to the hospital, where my father was resting and receiving fluids. He was weak but alive. He'd apparently been calling for my brother for days, and, not having his cane or phone in his room, he had been unable to reach out to anyone else. I think the doctor had told him that my brother had passed, but nothing more. He showed no feeling about it. Maybe he was in shock or, as the doctor suggested, his precarious condition made it hard for him to process that kind of news. The whole ordeal had been very traumatic for him.

After a short visit, my sister and I decided to stop by the house to pick up some things for Dad. We planned to spend the night there. It was late; the rooms were dark, cluttered, and unclean. An ominous feel of death and decay pervaded the entire house. My brother's room was as the neighbor had found it: no sheets or blankets on the bed, a pillow on the floor, and a calendar on the wall, with the days marked off, right up to the day he died.

On the dining-room table we found two folders, one for my father, and one for my brother. They were laid out neatly, each containing a funeral plan: one that my father had purchased for himself and my mother when she was still alive, and one that my brother had purchased just weeks before—for himself. Inside my brother's folder, along with his funeral plan, was an envelope addressed to his son, with several hundred dollars and a handwritten suicide note in it, explaining how everyone, including his son, would be better off without him. He claimed to have some illness that he didn't want to burden people with. However, we never found records of doctor visits for this condition, nor any bills or records confirming anything but a heart condition that he'd had for years.

My sister and I looked at each other in horror. "It wasn't a heart attack," I mumbled. "No," she replied, her eyes reflecting the gravity of what we had just discovered.

"Did Dad know?" I wondered. I slumped down in a chair, trying to take it all in. "How did he do it?" I asked.

We assumed it was an overdose, but we never found any empty bottles of sleeping pills or other lethal drugs. We knew that, as a physical therapist, Jimmy could procure and administer a lethal dose of almost anything he wanted. He'd also been siphoning off some of my father's medications, which even Dad suspected. Whatever he took, it was clear he knew what he was doing.

His ex-wife planned a small memorial for him at a meeting hall in town. Very few people attended, mostly friends of my father's, and members of the immediate family—the same ones who had attended the intervention. His best friend was also there. Although the friend was an alcoholic himself, he had encouraged my brother to attend AA.

My nephew seemed lost as he walked around greeting people. He was not yet thirty, and now, he was fatherless. I could only imagine his pain. He never said anything, but I'm sure he noticed, as we all did, that no one from the hospitals where my brother had worked was in attendance. Maybe they didn't know about it. We kept everything low key. It saddened me that the one area of Jimmy's life in which he had done the most "good," was never publicly recognized. No speeches, not even an officiating minister. No graveside ceremony. No wake. People simply milled around as if not knowing what to do or say.

That was the only time I cried for my brother. Music was playing, and a song by the Doobie Brothers, one of my brother's favorite bands, came on the boombox. I was suddenly overcome with emotion. I tried to remember the things about him that I liked—his sense of humor, his love of oldies music, his taking us all out on his boat—but my tears were as much about our lack of closeness, as they were about losing him. *Why* were we never close? I wondered, was it our different personalities or interests? Or, was it something more systemic, something in the way we were raised that fostered distance between us? It all seemed so senseless, surreal, and tragic. It didn't have to end like this.

Because my nephew declined an autopsy, the cause of death was never confirmed. He didn't want it recorded as a suicide, perhaps out of shame, denial, or an attempt to protect his father's reputation. After all, obituaries print the cause of death, and this was a small town. Everyone would know how my brother had died. Instead, the obituary was as simple and nondescript as the memorial. None of us reported the contents of Jimmy's suicide note.

I have no idea if my father had known how my brother died before he, himself, died. Ironically, he passed away the same day as my brother's memorial, exactly a week after the neighbors had found them both. He died in the nursing home to which he'd been released after leaving the hospital. He had been too ill to return home. My sister and I sat with Dad as he lay dying. We kept requesting hospice care, which would have enabled him to receive adequate pain medication. It was finally granted a few hours before he passed. Jimmy's son and ex-wife joined us during this time, and my own son arrived from Berkeley to see his grandfather before he died.

Dad's funeral was held at a picturesque church on a hillside north of town, overlooking the ocean. It was in stark contrast to my brother's memorial. Lifelong friends my father had not outlived were in attendance, as well as people from his church, and from the many organizations to which he belonged. Everyone talked highly and lovingly of him. The minister officiated, and many people, including my sister and I, gave speeches in his honor. He was even given a naval gun salute for having served during World War II. People told stories and wept. I didn't cry that day.

When I think about my brother's suicide now, having researched the risk factors of suicide in the intervening years, I recognize many of those factors as contributors to the tragedy of his life, and his death. I will address them in more detail later, but to name a few, they include suffering from a disability, physical or emotional; substance abuse; shame; despair; hopelessness that things will change; lack of financial or emotional resources; inability or unwillingness to seek help; and lack or diminishment of emotional support (either real or perceived). Jimmy's anger masked all these factors, further discouraging the potential for real help. His self-imposed taboo against having or sharing authentic feelings isolated him not only from others, but also from himself, leading him to self-destruct on the inside before taking his physical life.

As mentioned earlier, my brother's death was not my first experience with suicide. My father-in-law had also committed suicide, first by drinking alcoholically, and then by running the exhaust in the car to asphyxiate himself. I had gone to his funeral.

A family friend (I'll call Stanley) also killed himself. He was an extraverted, charismatic individual, who belonged to my parents' church, and babysat my little sister from time to time. He was well respected in town and thoroughly enjoyed life, or seemed to. Everyone liked him, including me.

One day, my mother told me, "Stanley died. He committed suicide."

I didn't understand how that could be, given all I knew about Stanley. That was all that was said. Mother didn't elaborate.

Suicide Up Close and Personal

I knew Stanley had bipolar disorder, something I subsequently learned my ex-husband had as well, although I had not known it when we were married. He was diagnosed later, when he had sought treatment for PTSD. Apparently, my ex-husband had also considered suicide, putting a gun to his head after we separated.

Before any of these events, my mother had made her Mother's Day suicidal gesture. Neither my brother nor I had done anything special for her. My mother naturally felt unappreciated. My dad tried to reassure her, but suddenly, in an uncharacteristically emotional moment, she burst into tears, marched into the bathroom, and took a razor to her wrist. I don't know if she even broke the skin. My father stopped her, and then yelled at us for having made her do it. He must surely have been terrified by her behavior. So were we. She had always been the rock of the family, practical, stoic, always in control. But she'd lost it for a moment, and whether it was to make a point, or get attention, we all got the message. I never again forgot Mother's Day, and she never again made a gesture like that. Maybe it scared her, too.

In any case, the whole thing was swept under the rug, like everything else, never to be spoken of again. I sometimes wondered if things might have been different had we talked openly about these things—Stanley's suicide, my mother's suicidal gesture, and even my own adolescent depression—and received help to understand these events in an honest, compassionate, and informative way. It is often what is not conscious that seems fated to be acted out.[1] In my family, a lot was acted out rather than being made conscious.

My Story

Sitting in a folding chair at a last-minute memorial for my brother, I couldn't help but think back thirty-five years to the day when I had made a suicide attempt of my own. Jimmy's story could have been mine. Like him, I'd made the attempt after a failed career, and the loss of significant relationships. I was thirty years old. What led up to my suicide attempt was not a single incident, but a lifetime of shame and perceived failures.

I married my high-school sweetheart at nineteen and was divorced at twenty-six after my husband twice left me. During that time, I desperately fought to finish my education, first in theater arts, and then in psychology. I subsequently got my Master's Degree in education and became a teacher. Then, I met a man who two years later followed me to Boston, where we both pursued careers in writing. Unable to make any significant inroads in publishing, we returned to California, where he, too, suddenly left me. This was a pattern that seemed to repeat itself along themes that began in childhood, a childhood I shared with my brother. This is the story of how it all unfolded.

Childhood

The family constellation into which I entered the world as the eldest child differed significantly from the one into which Jimmy was born three years later. Unlike him, I was cradled in the arms of an extended family during my first two years. I received much attention, not just from my parents, but from my grandparents, an aunt, an uncle, and a cousin.

Suicide Up Close and Personal

We were all poor, yet we spent our days together in my paternal grandparents' small, two-bedroom house in downtown Los Angeles. My parents took up residence in a trailer behind the house. My aunt and cousin on my father's side joined us during the day while my uncle was at work. Both my aunt and my father had grown up in this house during the Great Depression. My grandfather was now retired, so he, too, was home, mostly sitting in his rocker listening to the radio and barking orders at my grandmother, who dutifully waited on him. My grandmother was born of Swedish immigrants, while my grandfather was somehow related to Thomas Jefferson, or so the story goes. My father worked the night shift, so he was also around during the day. It was he who took me on outings to the store and on errands, as well as to fun activities, such as a play day at a local amusement park. My first word was *bye-bye*, a term for going someplace with Daddy.

Before she married my father, my mother, the daughter of an Irish alcoholic, dropped out of community college and took off with a friend on an adventure to Alaska, bobbing in and out of bars with a truant officer on their heels. They found part-time waitressing jobs, and lied about their age. When she returned, she was ready to settle down with my father, who had served in the Navy during World War II, now held a job, and was crazy about her—something that never waned during their fifty years of marriage.

By the time my brother was born, we were living in a duplex owned by my maternal grandmother, who occupied the unit next door. My grandmother had divorced my grandfather before my mother left for Alaska. That might have been why my mother wanted to get away: the divorce had been hard on her.

When we moved to the duplex, my father got a better job, the one he had until his retirement. This meant he worked days, and was no longer available to me as he had been. Meanwhile, my mother was preoccupied in caring for my brother, who suffered from problems with his legs for which he wore a brace during infancy. She was a nervous mother, a trait that had been less noticeable when so many other adults had been around to help her at my other grandmother's house. I was not allowed to lift or hold my baby brother because my mother feared something would happen to him. I interpreted this as a vote of no confidence. As I would later learn, Mother needed to be in control of everything. Much of her energy went into obsessive cleaning, mediated by chain smoking and, as I grew older, evening sips of wine or beer.

During that time, I experienced what I can only describe as a deep sense of aloneness, which is ironic given that for the first two years of my life I had almost never been alone. Maybe that was the problem. Upon reflection, I realize that the broken connection with my father, and the anxiety of my mother, as well as the lack of affection and need for control that she exhibited, impacted me in ways that contributed to a sense of abandonment and low self-esteem. My relationships with men were particularly affected. The fact that she would tell me I was so selfish that no man would want me probably didn't help.

My father's form of shaming was different from my mother's. It felt more like rejection. Once I was old enough to speak up, he castigated me for my high-spirited, but sensitive, nature. Perhaps, I reminded him of his more outspoken sister, whom he blamed for upsetting his own childhood household rather than attributing the cause of the family tension to his domineering father. Dad's model of feminine strength was his stoic and mostly passive Swedish mother, whom he idolized. He felt threatened by any show of emotions, something both his sister and I were able to express, but a trait about which both of us learned to feel much shame. My father often described me as "overly dramatic" and accused me of instigating conflicts. My punishment was to go to my room.

When I was a child, my room became a kind of torture chamber. It's where I internalized my learned sense of badness. My mother often consigned me to my room as well, urging me to "think about" how bad I was. If I didn't think long and hard, my time would be extended.

"I don't think you've thought about it enough," she would say when I apologized and begged to come out. I took my punishment seriously, ingesting her pronouncements of me like a slow poisoning of my soul.

As a therapist, I have since learned the importance of early childhood experiences with caregivers. The experience of being wanted, appreciated, or loved gets internalized, as does a sense of being a burden or thorn to our caregivers and intimate others. The messages we internalize determine how grounded we are in life. The way our feelings are mirrored back to us becomes the basis of our sense of self. During my infancy, I was loved and valued, but by three years old, I had become the family scapegoat, feeling abandoned and unworthy.

I would not describe myself as an unhappy child; nor was I happy, the way some kids are from birth. I didn't really give it much thought until later when I experienced unhappiness in a conscious way. On the surface, I was like any other child: smart, imaginative, creative, and eager to please. What set me apart was my sensitivity. In kindergarten, I would eat lunch alone on a bench. I was very shy. I looked forward to starting school and begged my mother to teach me the alphabet when I was three years old. I started school before I was five, but it was a disappointment. Rather than learning to read and write, we painted and played games. Also, I was often alone due to my painful shyness. My only friend was the boy next door, who was a year older.

When I was six, we moved to a house in Burbank, a suburb of Los Angeles. During elementary school, kids made fun of me because I cried if I received a bad grade, (less than an A) or if someone hurt my feelings. Most of my tormentors were boys. Looking back, I think they were uncomfortable with their own feelings. Making fun of others made them feel better. Although I had friends, I never felt I fit in. I always related to other kids who were bullied or made fun of, regardless of the reason.

When I was twelve, we moved again, this time to the Central Coast northwest of Los Angeles. For my thirteenth birthday, I invited several kids from my new school to my party, many of whom I barely knew but wanted to know better. Almost no one showed up. I subsequently fell into a mood that my mother called "depression," which seemed, from her description, to be a form of unhappiness. It was then that I wondered if I had always been a little depressed. What she was describing didn't feel temporary.

In retrospect, I realize that I'd been suffering for years from low self-esteem and perhaps a deep sadness, the source of which I couldn't quite pinpoint. It was as if I didn't really belong in this world and in this family. Even as a child living in the duplex, I felt that this world wasn't really my home, that there was another place I belonged, a place I needed to return to—or find. Not surprisingly, my favorite story as a child was the *Ugly Duckling*, a story about not belonging and searching for one's true flock.

By my junior year in high school, I discovered one attribute onto which I could hang my sense of worth. It was my ability to excel in school. I'd always done well academically, except when we moved the first time, and again during junior high when I was trying hard to adjust to my new surroundings. Transitions were always difficult. For the most part, I felt invisible. I had a few friends and didn't date much in high school, but I was active in Thespians, and wrote a lot of poetry. I decided then that I would major in theater and English in college.

In my senior year, I met the man who would become my husband. He literally picked me out of a crowd at a town-hall dance, swept me onto the dance floor, and into his life. He was four years older, and known to be a handsome and charming flirt—not the type to be attracted to me! He seemed out of my league. Yet, we were inseparable after that night. A pair of opposites. In him, I felt I found the love and acceptance for which I had always longed.

Nevertheless, in September, I left for college as planned, discovering in the San Francisco of the late 1960s, a place where I finally fit in. For the first time, I felt truly alive. If the people there weren't my true flock, they were close. I loved school; I loved the political activity and the sense of freedom from the sources of shame with which I'd grown up. My boyfriend came up to visit as much as he could, but a year into my education, he got drafted and was deployed to Vietnam. Before he left, we became engaged.

Marriage and Divorce

When my fiancé was given the opportunity to meet me in Hawaii for a period of R&R midway through his tour of duty in Vietnam, my parents helped plan a small wedding in Oahu—the guests were only my parents, and my aunt and uncle on my mother's side, with whom my parents vacationed the week before our wedding. Our wedding offered my mother the opportunity to finally go to Hawaii, something my father was less keen on. No one from my fiancé's family attended.

Because of the infamous Tet Offensive in Vietnam in February of 1968, my fiancé, who was fighting outside Saigon, was unable to get a flight out. His R&R was called off at the last minute, at least temporarily. I received a call from the Red Cross notifying me of this change. I wasn't told whether my fiancé was dead or alive, only that I would be contacted when flights resumed. I remained in San Francisco until the Red Cross called again, informing me that my fiancé would be boarding a flight to Hawaii the next day. But my parents were due to return home that same next day from the big island of Hawaii. By the time I called their hotel to give them the news, they had already left for the airport. I then called the airline, which, in 1966, did things the "old-fashioned way". They slipped a note from me into my parents' ticket envelope, which read, "I am flying into Oahu tomorrow. Change of plans. Call me." By the time my parents received the note, they were already boarding the plane back to California. Their luggage had to be removed from the plane on the tarmac, and transferred to another plane headed back to Oahu, where they reserved a hotel, and notified my father's employer that he needed to take a few more days off. I flew into Oahu the next day to meet them.

My mother always felt confident that my fiancé would make it to Oahu, but by the time he arrived, another three days had passed. By then, my aunt and uncle had already left the island and were headed home. We were married in a huge, glassed-in cathedral, rimmed by tropical plants that dwarfed the minister, the organist, my parents, and my husband and me—the only people in attendance. That day, as if symbolically, I lost my voice and had to whisper my vows. The next day, my parents flew home, and my husband and I honeymooned for three days before he returned to Vietnam—his leave cut short because of the Tet Offensive. I returned to San Francisco to finish my sophomore year of college. When the semester ended in June 1968, I returned to my parents' house in southern California to await my husband's return. I thought I'd resume school once he was discharged. Nevertheless, leaving San Francisco, I wept as I watched the college, and the city I had so loved, disappear into the distance.

When my husband returned from Vietnam a couple of months later, he and I drove to Colorado, where he served out his remaining time in the Army. After six months, we moved back to California, but I didn't return to college. He wasn't interested in an academic life. He called working "the school of hard knocks," the only education a person needed. While stateside, the Army trained him for work selling mutual funds, and connected him with an employer in Oakland, California. There, overlooking the Bay, I could view the city—San Francisco-- that once held such promise for me. Instead, I worked as a secretary in an iron-works company in Oakland.

Neither my husband nor I made much money, so my husband applied for a job in Sacramento with a paint company, spurred on by our apartment having been robbed in Oakland. In Sacramento, I got another secretarial job, this time working for an insurance company; but I began taking classes, first at the community college and then at the state university there. I changed my major to psychology. I was in the middle of my first semester there when my husband suddenly left, not explaining why. He didn't even pack his things. He'd been drinking heavily, and later I learned that many Vietnam vets suffered from PTSD, including him. At the time, however, I accepted the marital failure as mine alone.

Unable to support myself without his income, I was forced to move back home with my parents, filled with a deep sense of confusion and grief—assuming I just wasn't worthy. If I were, my husband wouldn't have left. I had believed he deeply loved me. I never considered that maybe he was running from something inside himself. I only knew that I'd failed to make him happy, and that thought filled me with shame. Some of that feeling I attribute to the many warnings my mother made as I was growing up about how I wouldn't be able to keep a man if I didn't stop being so selfish and self-centered. It was reminiscent of the shame I had felt from the messages I ingested so many times when I was sent to my room as a child.

Fortunately, I was able, with the help of student loans, and the emotional support of my aunt and cousin, to resurrect my life and attend UCLA. My aunt and cousin still lived in Los Angeles where they resided since I was a baby living in the trailer behind my grandparent's house. We had always been very close. They suggested that I stay with them so that I could commute to school. I hadn't expected to live there. My uncle had died of cancer when my cousin was sixteen, and it was just the two of them now, so they were happy to have me. My aunt, cousin, and I had not lived together since I was two years old, when we all occupied my grandmother's house. Now, their humble home felt familiar and safe. They let me stay rent free, and when not in school, I worked. It was a major turning point for me.

After two years, I graduated cum laude with a degree in psychology. At UCLA, I met someone new—also in the psychology department—who encouraged me to finalize my divorce and go on to get my PhD. I was on course to do just that when my estranged husband sought reconciliation. My new boyfriend tried to convince me to stay with him instead. But I couldn't. I reunited with my husband, believing I was still in love with him. For him to want me back meant that I was lovable after all.

It is often the case with young women who have not yet developed a strong enough sense of self, that they look outside themselves for validation and a sense of worth. They make what Jungian analyst, Clarissa Pinkola Estés, in *Women Who Run With the Wolves*, calls "a bad bargain," trading their true self for the love of a man or material wealth, security, or some other addiction. I had not yet read the book, nor had my aunt, but she expressed disappointment about my decision. She disapproved of the way my husband had left me, and she made no secret of her feelings. Unlike the rest of my family, she never blamed me for his leaving. She saw in him what I could not, maybe because she, too, suffered all her life from low self-esteem and unrealized potential. She was unable to find her own strength during her lifetime, but she desired it for me, and believed that I could break the cycle.

She was right, of course, but I made the wrong choice, nonetheless. I followed my heart instead of my true self. I knew I was smart, but I lacked the kind of intelligence that made my mother so strong. She was rational, practical, and detail oriented. She was capable of expressing strong opinions and arguing her point forcefully. She was also critical and lacked other qualities, such as imagination, intuition, and warmth, that I would later embrace and come to value in myself. Meanwhile, she was the standard of intelligence for me. Her brand of smarts is what attracted my father, and it was what I believed most men wanted: someone rational, not emotional—logical, not intuitive.

By returning to my husband, I thought I'd be redeemed—proved worthy after all! However, two years later, when I applied to graduate school, he left me again, this time for good. We finalized the divorce when I was twenty-six. I felt devastated. Nevertheless, I continued my education; I obtained a Master's Degree in Special Education and became a special-education teacher. I gave up on acting and writing when I got married, thinking that teaching would be a more reliable way to make a living. I taught in preschools and private special-education schools during college, and liked it.

After finishing my Master's, I was offered a job with the Los Angeles County schools teaching kids in juvenile hall. It was the first time in my life when I was making enough money to live on my own. It was also when I met Josh (not his real name). We were both teachers. In addition, we both liked to write, and worked on several writing projects together. I felt that I'd found a real partner in Josh, that our relationship had all the ingredients missing in my marriage. Only one thing was absent: commitment. He'd never been married, and was not ready to commit to one woman. In fact, he encouraged me to see other men in addition to him. I tried hard to be a more "modern" woman for him by dating other men. But over time, it became wearing. We saw each other on the weekends when he wasn't with other women. We lived a few blocks apart. We taught at the same school, often in the same classroom. There was no way to avoid him.

Meanwhile, my older male cousin in Boston encouraged me to visit him there, even to move back east if I wanted to write. There were plenty of opportunities. Since my relationship with Josh wasn't developing and my teaching position was proving not to be fulfilling, after all, I decided to take my cousin up on his offer, and move to Boston. I still had not fully grieved my husband; and, looking back, I now believe that I ran away from Josh to avoid another heartbreak. I thought that I was moving toward greater possibilities. I was actually headed for another heartache.

Broke and Broken in Boston

In Boston, I managed to write a few articles for a liberal-leaning newspaper, even though, try as I might, I could not land a full-time job. Seeing that I'd had some success, Josh decided to join me. He, too, had become disillusioned with the teaching job at juvenile hall. Between substitute teaching gigs and food stamps, we eked out a living in an apartment furnished by Goodwill and items left on the street.

Initially, I felt there was hope for the relationship, and my career. We had become a couple, who shared and supported each other's career choices. We even wrote articles together. We both worked as substitute teachers to augment our income, but it wasn't enough. Eventually, the financial struggle, and career failures, took a toll. Neither of us could make a living; nor could we establish a social circle. Boston was a hard city to fit into. We felt isolated, and a little lost.

After a couple of years, we each applied to graduate schools in California: Josh in creative writing, myself in journalism. Neither of us was accepted into the graduate schools we applied to—he to San Francisco State College, my alma mater, and me to U.C. Berkeley, just across the Bay. Money was running out, and our relationship was faltering. Josh turned his depression into shaming comments about me that I could not defend against. In many ways, he projected aspects of his bipolar mother onto me. In particular, he disliked my clinginess and fear of abandonment, as well as my jealousies and emotionality—something he had once found attractive. His coolness further activated my abandonment fears, which resulted in more shaming, and even more insecurity. Finally, we agreed to return to California, having no idea what we would do when we got there.

We'd exhausted our funds by the time we arrived, so we decided to camp out at my parents' house. They usually spent summers out of town, at another division of my father's business where he covered for employees who were on vacation. Only my younger sister was at home with my brother, who had finished school, and was working as a physical therapist. Josh suggested we drive up to Monterey to see a friend, and to check out the job market there. However, Josh turned increasingly cold and distant on the trip. The fissures between us seemed to have widened under all the stress. I could feel him leaving even before he was gone.

One morning, Josh suddenly left, just as my ex had, expressing that he was done with the relationship and wanted to separate. He determined that I would go back to my parent's house, and he would drive on to LA to live with friends there. The relationship was over. This felt like my worst nightmare, the thing I most feared—that Josh, too, would leave me, and I'd end up back at my parents' house at the age of thirty.

On the Greyhound bus back to my parents' place, memories of my failed relationships flooded me. I remembered my mother urging me to be more "bubbly" like the other girls at school, and warning that, if I didn't change, I'd never find a man to love me. I thought about my father's shaming comments, and his preference for sensible, sweet women who were perky and positive. I was neither. It was despairing to find myself trapped once again in the small home town that held so many bad memories for me. I had no friends, no money, and nowhere to escape the depression that seemed to enfold me like a thick, black fog. I was drowning. This time, I didn't see a way out. So many losses in such a short time. So many disappointments. So many failures.

Then I learned that, adding salt to the wound, my ex-husband had moved back to town with his new wife. Surely, I would run into him at some point. I felt sick inside at the thought. My parents were due back home any day. My brother and sister knew what had happened to me. My brother seemed to take delight in my misfortune. My sister felt sad for me, but didn't know what to say or do. She was only seventeen, and a very young and inexperienced seventeen. Soon, my parents would know, too; in fact, the whole town would know! I had never felt so alone and ashamed. The house seemed haunted by ghosts. I couldn't sleep at night, and couldn't get out of bed during the day. I tried to drink myself to sleep on cheap wine that my parents kept around the house. It didn't help.

Desire to Die

Finally, I called our family physician. I explained to him what I was going through. I needed to sleep. He prescribed sleeping pills. I took one pill each evening, but the pills didn't offer much relief, and I still had to bear the days. I felt tormented by the destructive narratives I constantly fed myself, about myself. I replayed in my mind hurtful comments Josh and others had made about me When the pills were gone, I asked for more. This time, I planned to take them all. I didn't think about how my doctor's wife had committed suicide years before from an overdose, and how my own suicide might affect him. I didn't think about anything but ending the inner pain.

    I washed the pills down with some cheap wine for good measure, just as my father-in-law had done before asphyxiating himself. Before then, I would not have considered suicide as an option, but on that particular day, I felt it was the *only* option. I did not want to wake up; I could not bear to live in my own skin.

    As I lay waiting for the pills to take effect, I called a therapist I had seen briefly in Boston when things began to go awry with Josh and me, and with my career. I wanted her to know what had happened—the end of the story. I also wanted to hear a voice that was not shaming or angry, someone who could hear why I had made this choice, someone with compassion. I did not expect that there would be anything she could do to stop me, my being three thousand miles away, and having already ingested the pills. Calling her was my attempt at a suicide note, I suppose, but it needed to be spoken, not written. I wanted the last voice I heard to be a loving one.

My call to her was followed by a call she made to the local police, something I didn't realize was possible. I don't know how they knew where I was, but they apparently showed up at the door after I had passed out. My brother said I was fine, just a little drunk. He had seen me drinking earlier, but had no idea that I'd taken sleeping pills with the wine. I don't even know what he told them to reassure them or why I wasn't taken to the hospital. I think my brother may have called the doctor afterward, though.

As it turned out, the doctor anticipated my actions, and had prescribed a nonlethal dose. I awoke the next day, groggy, my arms stinging from burns apparently inflicted by a lit cigarette that I had been smoking. I had a dim awareness of what had happened, including the call to my therapist. To this day, there are many gaps in my memory of that time.

My brother greeted me the next morning with a critical and demeaning look, as if I had just proved everyone right. I was scum. Whether to protect or punish me, he had deactivated my car during the night and taken my keys. I wasn't going anywhere. He also told my parents what had happened. I would now live in a hell that was even worse than the one before my failed suicide attempt.

I can only imagine how the suicide of my doctor's wife a few years earlier had served to alert him to the potential for my own suicide. He must have heard in my voice the anguish I was feeling, and the desperation to end the pain. By anticipating my actions, he protected me from myself. I felt angry at him at the time, but, in retrospect, I consider him one of the angels who spared me from an untimely death.

Punishment in the Aftermath

When my parents returned home from their summer away, we didn't talk about my suicide attempt. They viewed my actions as me acting out and humiliating them; and it seemed that, after the attempt, my behavior gave them reason to think so. Left with no options for release, I began to connect with a deep anger inside, an anger at my parents that I began openly to express. I hated them for teaching me to hate myself. I hated them for not being there for me when I felt so alone and full of shame—shame they helped, in part, to create. They had always blamed me for my own misfortune, unable to grasp the complexities of cause and effect. Sometimes, they blamed my misfortune on my lack of faith in the Lord Jesus. If I were only more religious, things would turn out well for me.

I, on the other hand, felt that if I'd been loved, things would have gone better for me. I would have had more confidence; I wouldn't have ended up in relationships that were unsustainable; I would have felt more capable in my career choices. There was no warmth in the house, no one to hug me when life brought disappointments, hurt feelings, fears of being

Suicide Up Close and Personal

abandoned. My parents' reaction to all this rage was to further reject and abandon me. At one point, I got into an altercation with my father and slapped him, crying that I hated him. My mother, in turn, decided it was time for me to leave. Since I had nowhere to go, she found a women's shelter for me.

Her actions reminded me of what had happened to my cousin, Teri, with whom I'd lived while attending UCLA. Teri's mother, my aunt, had died from a brain tumor while visiting my parents before I moved to Boston. In fact, it was my aunt's death that had added impetus to my decision to make the move, out of the fear of living an unlived life, as she had. While I was in Boston, and after her mother's death, Teri stayed with my parents, having nowhere else to go. She had dropped out of school when she was a teenager due to bullying. Later, she got her GED, but she had no life skills, and never held down a real job. She was thirty when my aunt died.

My aunt and cousin had cleaned houses for income ever since my uncle died. In many ways, Teri was developmentally delayed, although intrinsically bright, with a memory like an elephant. In her grief at the loss of her mother, she began "acting crazy," as my mother called it, taking long walks at night with her mother's dog, and meeting strange men with whom she "made out" in front of the house. Mother could not abide such behavior, and demanded that Teri stop, threatening my father that "It's either her or me." My father reluctantly acquiesced, despite having promised his sister, my aunt, that he would care for Teri if anything happened to her mother. He could not make good on his promise.

Years earlier, my father had also failed to support me when my mother kicked me out while I lived with them after I returned from college at San Francisco State, until my husband came back from Vietnam. Believing myself to be an adult then, I had attempted to be honest about some of my feelings, including my treatment as a child. I figured that since I was now married, I could express my true feelings without punishment. But my mother didn't appreciate my honesty. She felt that college had made me insolent and disrespectful, and said I had to leave. I moved in with my mother-in-law across town for a few weeks until my husband arrived. Now married, we moved to Colorado, then Oakland, and finally Sacramento, before the marriage ultimately fell apart.

Now, at thirty, I was kicked out again. Ironically, the shelter my mother found was for abused women. It had no hot water, so residents boiled water on the stove to take showers, and everyone cooked together. Some of the women did not speak English, but we seemed to share a common emotional language, the language of shame, rejection, and despair.

After several weeks, I begged my parents to let me come home. I apologized for my misbehavior and promised not to bring up any angry feelings. I knew that I had to get back on my feet, and I couldn't from a shelter. I needed to go home. My parents agreed to let me move back into their home, at least until I could find a job. I said goodbye to my new soul sisters at the shelter. They would not be going home any time soon. But then, neither was I, really. Not yet. Not to a home of my own, that is, which is the only *real* home. I needed to come home to myself.

One of the first things I did, was consult a psychiatrist, who prescribed medication. My parents paid for it, and my younger brother was entrusted to give me my daily dose, lest I overdose—an irony, given how he later did just that himself.

Suicide Up Close and Personal

After I told my story to the psychiatrist, he asked to see the whole family, especially my parents. He felt that the problem was systemic, that the entire family was broken. My parents declined, saying any "problem" was *my* problem, not theirs. The psychiatrist, in response, suggested I find a way to leave town. He cautioned that if I remained there, living with my parents, I would probably be dead in a year. Most likely, I would make another suicide attempt. The environment, and my relationship with my parents, were psychologically too lethal, and my ego too fragile. He explored with me a plan for my life going forward.

I mentioned still wanting to be a writer. I had degrees in psychology and special education, but I felt a degree in journalism might help me land a writing job. He encouraged me. Initially, I had no idea how to accumulate the money to leave. I then remembered that my parents had a life insurance policy they had taken out when I was born. Since it was paid up, and I was an adult, I could cash it in. It would give me a thousand dollars. If I applied to school, I could pay for an apartment while I looked for work near campus. I had a plan now, and support.

Meanwhile, I found a part-time job working in a local department store. I also applied to my old high school to substitute teach. It was humbling. My sister still attended school there. I substituted for some of her classes. I couldn't believe how far I'd fallen. But with the psychiatrist's confidence in me, I earned enough money to leave town. Both my psychiatrist, and my family physician, served as angels during the darkest time of my life.

Before leaving town, I asked my ex-husband if we could meet for coffee and discuss what had happened in our marriage, hoping for some kind of closure. He refused. I felt further rejected and ashamed, but I had known ahead of time that there was a chance that our relationship would end that way.

Six months after attempting suicide, I got into my car, and drove away for good. I moved back to Los Angeles, where I shared an apartment with a perfect stranger, and obtained a part-time job while enrolling in the journalism program at a local university. From that point, I began the long journey of recovery. Enroute, I became a therapist, and later a Jungian analyst. I continued to write.

Post Suicide

While I never made another attempt at suicide (true of a many people who attempt suicide), I cannot say that the thought, even the pull, of suicide completely abated. There were times when the feeling, like a demon from the deep, would rise up in me, and like Odysseus facing the pull of the Sirens on his return voyage from Troy, I would have to tie myself psychologically to the mast, and not give in to the sirens of death.

Later, in analysis, I discovered the psychological meaning in my suicidal gesture. I realized that I had confused physical death with symbolic death. Yes, *something* in me needed to die—old ideas about how selfish and crazy I was, beliefs I clung to about love, and an insistence on finding the happy ever after—but it wasn't my *physical* life that needed to end.

In my work as an analyst, I've learned that in each person who contemplates suicide, there always exists a part that wants to die, and a part that wants to live. To live, however, requires that one "let die" those elements of the personality that are not life affirming. In my case, it was the shame, which I will talk about later. There was also a naïve, puella aspect to my personality that I clung to the way Persephone in the Greek myth clings to her innocent, maiden self—a very young part of the self that has not yet learned the meaning of suffering.

Jung talks about the *puer* in men and the *puella* in women, which in Latin means "boy" and "girl," respectively. The puella refers to a woman who is inwardly insecure, depressed, disembodied, and childlike. She often has a young, and romantic view, of life. In myths, she is characterized by the maiden, uninitiated and naïve. That's how I was in my twenties. Having married so young, and holding onto an overly romantic idea of life, I refused to accept life's inherent cruelty. It was, in part, a defense against the pain of the shame I carried, but it was unsustainable. I needed to be initiated into an acceptance of suffering as necessary to growth. In that respect, my suicide attempt served as a kind of initiation ritual, one that I survived.

Before concluding, I want to emphasize that I grew up in a family that could not handle feelings, especially strong feelings. Even positive emotions, such as excitement, needed to be tamped down. My brother almost never expressed emotions other than anger and contempt. He never said, "I love you." When a person suppresses all of their so-called negative feelings, the positive ones get buried along with them—even though, at gatherings with friends or family, the person's behavior might seem normal.

I don't blame my parents for my suicide attempt, any more than I blame the men in my life. I don't blame any individual person or event, but I do understand how they all converged to create a potentially lethal combination. Instead, I am aware of the emotional and psychological limitations that motivated their behavior, as well as my own at the time. I am grateful to the "angels" who, without knowing it, played a role in my transformation, and eventual healing. In addition to the family physician and the town psychiatrist, I have been blessed with gifted therapists and analysts, as well as friends. During my lifetime, there were many angels who lit the path for me to follow. Sadly, that did not happen for my brother. I recognize that for some, that longed-for rebirth never arrives, at least not in this lifetime.

As I have mentioned, no one in my family was curious or talked about my attempted suicide. It was just that: an attempt. I didn't die. My father called me a survivor (when he wasn't calling me dramatic or selfish), something I resented because it didn't acknowledge the suffering I endured before, during, and after the suicide attempt. He never asked why I wanted to kill myself or what he could do to help. He simply said, "Time heals all wounds." But it didn't, and it doesn't. Healing is not a consequence of time and staying silent. Healing comes from its opposite. It comes from talking about it—a lot. And, the healing continues.

2
THE WHO, HOW, AND WHY OF SUICIDE: AN OVERVIEW

> *The most significant problem with risk models is that they rely almost entirely on statistical methods describing prevalence and association, which tell us what may be related to suicidal behavior, but not what causes it.*
> —Anna S. Mueller et al.

My brother's death left me with many questions, not only about his death, but about suicide in general. I wondered how prevalent death by suicide was in the United States, and around the world, and whether its frequency had increased or decreased over the years. I wondered if there was any data on those who attempted, or thought about, suicide but didn't in fact kill themselves. Who was more at risk for suicide, and had the risk factors changed over time? In short, I was curious about the statistics of suicide, and whether my own experiences and those of my family, friends, and clients were similar in any ways. Was I alone in my experience, or could other people relate?

I reviewed hundreds of studies and statistical analyses over several years. The more I read, the more curious I became. I discovered that the answers were more complex than I thought. For example, the statistics on suicide were not static; they were ever changing, so much so that when I was ready to cite them, many had already shifted—as they continue to do. Furthermore, the conclusions that experts drew from these statistics differed widely. I nevertheless recognized some trends and patterns. In fact, the generalities illuminated the issue more than the specific numbers did. What follows is data that stood out:

- In 2020, suicide was the nation's tenth leading cause of death, and it has hovered around that number for many years. During the 2019 coronavirus (COVID-19) pandemic, suicide dropped to the eleventh leading cause of death due to so many COVID-19 related deaths. As the death rate from the pandemic dropped, stresses increased—and suicides increased, too.[1]
- Suicide percentages tend to go up during times of crisis, such as during the Great Depression, but tend to go down during times of war. This is because the actual numbers of deaths by suicide are always relative to other causes of death. Over time, though, the rate of suicidal deaths has steadily risen—since 1999, for instance, by 35 percent.[2]
- Although more women than men attempt suicide, more men than women succeed in killing themselves, but that gap is narrowing.
- Men tend to use firearms, and other more lethal means, to kill themselves than do women, which accounts for men's attempts being more successful.

The Who, How, and Why of Suicide: An Overview

- Worldwide, the number of suicides has increased in the last forty-five years, and although rates of suicide in the United States are high, some other countries have much higher rates. In 2021, South Korea had the highest number of suicides among the thirty-eight countries in the Organization for Economic Cooperation and Development, with twenty-six out of every 100,000 people taking their lives. "In contrast to the global downward trend, South Korea's suicide rate has nearly doubled over the past two decades."[3]
- Certain minority groups, such as Native Americans, have higher suicide rates than whites, but Asians and Hispanics (especially women) have even lower rates. Again, the relative percentages among groups tend to change from time to time. For example, suicide among blacks decreased during the pandemic, but have increased since then.
- The rates for suicide among young people have been increasing over the years, and yet the rate among the elderly remains among the highest in the country.
- Areas in the United States with high rates of gun ownership and substance abuse, combined with low access to mental-health services, tend to have among the highest rates of suicide. This has implications both for ethnic groups and for socio-economic class.
- Certain occupations have higher rates of suicide than others. A select group of blue-collar workers, and those in the medical professionals, especially doctors, have high rates of suicide, as do policemen and firefighters. Gender in professions has an impact as well. Women in

certain high-stress jobs have higher rates of suicide than men in those professions.
- In general, the risk for suicide is higher among people with severe mental illness.
- Gender minority groups have higher rates of suicide than heterosexuals.

These findings offered me a framework for beginning to investigate the subject more deeply. I was interested in the rates of suicide worldwide, as well as rates related to age, sex, ethnicity, and occupation in this country. I looked at contributing factors such as socio-economic status, geographical location, neurobiology, and genetics, as well as the relationships among suicide and violence, substance abuse, and homicide. In addition, I compared rates of completed suicides with those of attempted suicides and people who seriously considered killing themselves. The results of my investigation appear in appendix B.

Meanwhile, a word about statistics in general. Statistics can tell us a great deal. For example, they can reveal the number of actual suicides, as well as the number of people who attempt, or even consider it, based on available data. They can indicate, but not definitively predict, what groups of people are more likely to kill themselves according to age, sex, race, socio-economic class, etc. From this information, experts can proffer hypotheses, devise theories, and design suicide-prevention programs.

Emile Durkheim, a French sociologist, was the first to compile statistics specifically on suicide, which he published in 1897 in a book called *Le Suicide: Étude de sociologie* (Suicide: A Study in Sociology). Since then, it has been the province of governments to compile those statistics, and for academicians, and others, to make sense of them. This is a complicated endeavor, however, because numbers can't tell us everything.

What statistics cannot explain, for example, is the unique stories, and complex factors that combine to drive a particular individual to end his or her life. Nor can statistics prove the existence of any cause-and-effect relationship. They can't conclude, for example, that because a person is depressed, he or she is likely to commit suicide, or that people who own a gun are more likely than not to kill themselves with it. Yet, we know from the available data that a white male, diagnosed with depression, and a gun owner, presents a combination that, along with certain other circumstantial factors, may place him or her at higher risk for suicide than someone lacking that combination.

In general, statistics reveal upward and downward trends, the reasons for the trends we can only speculate about. The numbers also tell us how many people were diagnosed with a mental disorder at the time they died, but they can't assume that the illness caused the suicide. They reveal how many people who committed suicide were divorced, wartime veterans, alcoholics, or drug addicts, but they can't tell us which factor(s) actually led to their death.

We know, for instance, that high schoolers who misuse opioids are at a higher risk for suicidal behavior, but we don't know why each person in the sample chose to take opioids in the first place, and what impact each of those factors had on their decision to kill themselves. Social and psychological factors such as peer pressure, problems at home, poor self-esteem, chronic depression, trauma, or poverty might have played a role.

Studies have also found correlations between impulsivity and suicide, but they are just that—correlations. In young people, the added factor of depression, abuse, trauma, bullying, mental illness, poverty, and racism may increase the likelihood of suicide, and, together, produce an even higher correlation, but we don't know which of these factors put a person over the edge.

According to one study, between 1999 and 2018, the total rate of suicide in the United States increased 35 percent; some states had higher suicide rates than others, among them states in the western third of the country. Rates were lowest in the northeast.[4] We can speculate on why that would be, but we can't assume that someone in Boston is less likely to commit suicide than someone in, say, Taos, New Mexico. Appendix A offers an example of how statistics can be confusing by looking at how Seattle came to be labeled "the saddest city in the country."

Given all the caveats, a deeper dive is offered in appendix B, which expands on each of the following categories: suicide around the globe, suicides by age and sex, ethnicity and suicide, socio-economic factors in suicide, occupations with the highest rates of suicide, violence and suicide, attempted versus completed suicides, suicide and homicide, and the various means used to commit suicide, including the most lethal.

3

HISTORICAL ATTITUDES TOWARD SUICIDE

Suicide has been known in all cultures, every region and ethnic group. Throughout history, the first recorded suicides were committed by Pyramus and Thisbe, who were lovers that died in Babylonia, Persia, around 2000 BC.

—Saxby Pridmore et al.

While my suicide attempt, like those of other people, had its unique aspects, the act of suicide itself is universal and archetypal. Nevertheless, since the beginning of time, societies have varied in their attitudes about it, some rejecting it outright, no matter the circumstances. Some have made exceptions, whereby suicide, if not openly accepted, is at least tolerated. Others have openly endorsed suicide under certain conditions.

Among the earliest recorded suicides are those from Greek and Roman mythology, poetry, and drama. From them, we gain some insight into the thinking of early humanity regarding life and death, and suicide in particular. We can even divide these narratives into stories in which characters are motivated to commit suicide by certain critical events, as when a hero's actions bring catharsis or resolution to a crisis, or in which a character is seeking to avoid, alter, or prevent a dreaded occurrence, as is the case in many Greek tragedies.[1] In these narratives, both male and female characters commit suicide, although the specific motives and means are often different. In each case, though, suicide is regarded as virtuous if the act ensures one's honor and dignity.

During the Trojan War, for instance, Ajax, the great grandson of Zeus and the king of Salamis, took his own life after competing with the more powerful Odysseus for the armor of the hero Achilles. Ajax lost. Various versions of the story describe him as driven to kill himself by grief, anger, disappointment, and humiliation. According to some scholars, Ajax recognized that suicide was the only solution to end his shame and preserve his heroic identity.[2]

The death of Iphigenia is another example. While she didn't commit suicide in the traditional sense, Iphigenia, daughter of Agamemnon, allowed her father to sacrifice her to appease the goddess Artemis, who demanded the sacrifice. Iphigenia made the choice to die willingly, so that the Greek soldiers could continue their voyage to Troy unencumbered by strong winds.

Other famous examples: Following his murder of Julius Caesar, Brutus committed suicide after his army was defeated in war. Some say he fell on his sword, as was common then; others say he disemboweled himself. Defeat in war, and lost love, also motivated the deaths of Antony and Cleopatra—Antony by falling upon his sword when told she was dead, and she by allowing a poisonous snake to bite her after learning that she was about to lose her kingdom. For similar reasons, Shakespeare's Romeo and Juliet ended their lives—Romeo, after believing Juliet killed herself, she after learning that Romeo had in fact killed himself. The latter examples represent tragically romantic suicides, as well as heroic ones.

What all these stories together tell us is that, from the beginning of time, men and women have recognized death as a rational resolution to the problems of living. In contrast, contemporary Western culture views suicide mostly as an irrational act committed by emotionally unbalanced individuals, who possess an inherent weakness of character. For that reason, it is neither acceptable, nor justified, and certainly not heroic. One possible exception is assisted suicide: individuals experiencing severe physical pain and suffering from a terminal illness for which there is no chance of recovery may request assistance in dying. But even assisted suicide is not accepted by all segments of society.

The word *euthanasia*, which means putting someone out of their misery, comes from the Greek word for "good death" (*eu*: good and *thanatos*: death), referring to ending an individual's life if the person would otherwise endure severe, incurable suffering or disability.[3] (Another Greek term, *autocheir*, means to act with one's own hand, and implies that choice, planning, and self-determination are involved in one's death).[4] *Euthanasia* also derives from the seventeenth-century word *euthanasy*, referring to legally sanctioned mercy killings, which were first recorded in 1869.[5] Today, euthanasia is considered to be the "painless killing of a patient suffering from an incurable and painful disease or irreversible coma."[6]

Ending one's life due to illness, disability, or uselessness has a long history. Among nomadic tribes, a form of suicide called *senicide* was performed by family members who were too old to be helpful and thus presented a liability to the tribe's survival. It was customary for elders in such communities to remain behind voluntarily to die on their own. This was common among Innuit tribes, especially during times of famine. Senicide often involved making a bed in the ice for the long winter's sleep from which the person did not awaken.[7] According to Nordic urban legends, elderly people were said to leap, or be thrown, to their death from mountaintops. Similar forms of senicide were known to occur in Greek and Roman cultures, although by different names.[8] In Japan, a custom called *ubasute* was inflicted on infirmed or elderly relatives, who were carried to a mountain, or other desolate location, and left to die.[9]

In Hinduism, fasting to death was once acceptable for monks who had no more responsibilities to justify their existence. Again, it was not illness or physical suffering per se that prompted the taking of one's life but their age and uselessness in society. In India, a form of senicide called: *thalaikoothal*, has long been considered humane, and is still sometimes practiced in the southern Indian state of Tamil Nadu. The practice may, or may not, involve the active participation of the person dying. A story in the *Los Angeles Times* tells of an elderly woman who was poisoned by her daughter-in-law. The husband found his mother's lifeless body propped up in a chair when he returned from work. He claimed to harbor "no ill will" toward his wife for killing his mother, explaining, "My mother had been sick and in pain for 20 days and wasn't eating properly. I was thinking of doing it myself. It was time, and there wasn't enough food to go around."[10]

Similarly, a woman from the village of Subamma justified the practice as follows: "What else can they (the children) do if they see their parents suffering? At least they are offering their parents a peaceful death. It is an act of dignity because living like a piece of log for years is disrespectful for the elderly themselves, more than it is for us."[11]

The Los Angeles Times article reports that while some in India call the practice euthanasia, others consider it homicide. It notes that while thalaikoothal was traditionally practiced on people over fifty, some young people request it for themselves, even in cases of minor illnesses, while some old people are terrified of it, and may even flee when they get wind of it.[12]

In many cultures, from antiquity to the present, mercy killings, also called "easy deaths" or "dying for the right cause," have been considered acceptable ways to protect a person's honor, or prevent shame from being heaped upon the family. They have also been considered a means to avoid public humiliation, as in the case of warriors and prisoners of war.

A similar fate seemed to befall police officers following the January 6, 2021 insurrection, when three officers took their lives after they failed to hold back the mob of insurrectionists as they entered the United States Capitol. Whether the officers felt shame about failing their mission is unknown, but one could speculate that the resulting personal and public humiliation had a devastating effect on them.

History is filled with examples of heroic suicides, among them Mediterranean soldiers, who were known to go on killing sprees called *devotio*. A soldier would alert his comrades of his intention to kill in advance; then, the soldier would make his attack, killing as many of his opponents as possible, before being killed himself—or committing suicide.[13]

Mass suicides were also recorded among Celtic warriors who were besieged by Egyptian forces. In these cases, the soldiers chose suicide over surrender. In more modern times, so did many soldiers facing imprisonment by their captors during the two world wars, as well as spies who killed themselves rather than be taken by their enemies. Many of these suicides were performed to save face.

Japanese kamikaze pilots during World War II were hailed as patriots for driving their planes into enemy warships. In fact, Japan has a long history of sanctioning suicide, if not endorsing it. Samurai warriors, for example, were encouraged to commit suicide rather than fall into the hands of their enemies; and, their female family members were taught to commit *jigaki* (slitting the neck) to avoid capture and rape, thereby maintaining their chastity. Today, Japan still has one of the highest rates of adolescent suicide in the world.[14]

View of the Early Philosophers

Our own modern view of suicide can be traced back to the early Greek and Roman philosophers, and later to the emergence of Christianity. While some Greek and Roman philosophers viewed suicide through the lens of free will, claiming that individuals have the right to manage their own life as they see fit, others believed that choices about life and death were the sole province of the gods, much as we believe today, with the exception that, in keeping with the beliefs of Christianity, we look to one God instead of multiple ones.

The Greek philosopher, Socrates, who lived in Athens in the fifth century BCE, claimed that "a man . . . should not kill himself until the gods send some compulsion upon him."[15] At the same time, Socrates suggested that philosophers should not fear death, because philosophy itself is the "practice [of] dying," thus suggesting that death, and how one dies, is of utmost importance. Socrates maintained that, in the meantime, individuals would be wise to renounce earthly distractions such as bodily pleasure, pain, and riches, because the body not only impedes the soul's efforts to acquire knowledge, but is also inherently incapable of reason and, therefore, cannot pursue a philosophical life.[16]

Socrates seems to imply that meaning can only be known after death. Meanwhile, each person should wait to die until the gods call, for the gods are the bearers of greater knowledge and meaning, not humankind.

"We humans are in a kind of prison, and one must not release oneself or run away from it," Socrates said. "It is the gods who have regard for us and . . . we humans are the god's possessions." In some ways, this sounds a bit like the Christian belief, which also maintains that the decision to live or to die should be left to God.[17]

Plato, a student of Socrates, had a slightly different take on suicide. Plato believed that suffering from a fatal illness, or from dishonor, was a justifiable reason for committing suicide. Such deaths, he claimed, should not be a source of disgrace. In a sense then, suicide, under certain circumstances, was an acceptable way to die.

Citing Plato's *Laws*, the *Stanford Encyclopedia of Philosophy* states that for this acceptability of suicide, Plato recognized four conditions: "1) when one's mind is morally corrupt and one's character can therefore not be salvaged (*Laws* IX 854a3–5); 2) when the self-killing is done by judicial order, as in the case of Socrates; 3) when the self-killing is compelled by extreme and unavoidable personal misfortune; and 4) when the self-killing results from shame at having participated in grossly unjust actions (*Laws* IX 873c-d)."[18] Plato thought that, in such situations, suicide could be tolerated, but "it was otherwise an act of cowardice or laziness, undertaken by individuals too delicate to manage life's vicissitudes."[19] In this way, he agreed with Socrates, but he opened the door for people to make their own choice.

Aristotle, Plato's disciple, took a more strident view on suicide than even Socrates. Aristotle considered suicide a crime against oneself and one's country. Suicide, he said, was a wrong committed against the state or community, although he did not outline the exact nature of this wrong. Aristotle also agreed with Plato's philosophy that suicide is an act of cowardice in the face of life's adversities.[20] This thinking continues to this day.

It seems that both Plato and Aristotle were less concerned with the effect on a given individual, or even the gods, than they were on how a person's suicide affected society. As the *Stanford Encyclopedia of Philosophy* puts it, both Plato and Aristotle advised to "limit the justifications for suicide largely to considerations about an individual's social roles and obligations."[21]

In contrast, the Stoics, in the third century BC, believed that if the means to living a naturally flourishing life is not available, a person may be justified in committing suicide, regardless of the character or virtue of the individual in question. They, in fact, believed that suicide was "permissible" for wise people "in circumstances that might prevent them from living a virtuous life."[22]

Many Roman Stoics, including Seneca and Marcus Aurelius, claimed that death by one's own hand was "frequently more honorable than a life of protracted misery."[23] Seneca, who himself committed suicide, declared that the wise man is free to remove himself from life in the light of unfavorable fortune, "For mere living is not a good, but living well. Accordingly, the wise man will live as long as he ought, not as long as he can."[24]

Echoing that sentiment, Cicero is quoted as saying, "When a man's circumstances contain a preponderance of things in accordance with nature, it is appropriate for him to remain alive; when he possesses or sees in prospect a majority of the contrary things, it is appropriate for him to depart from life.[25]

Early philosophers, thus seemed to expand their view of suicide over time, considering not only the effect on society, or even the will of the gods, but also one's private feelings and experiences. Accordingly, if things got truly bad, an individual had the right to take his or her life. French writer and philosopher, Albert Camus, noted that "there is but one truly serious philosophical problem, and that is suicide. All the rest . . . comes afterwards."[26] In this statement, we may glean the idea that life and death are matters of value and choice based on one's philosophical perspective.

The Views of Christianity

In many ways, Christianity, which emerged in the mid-first century CE with the teachings of Christ, denied any excuse for suicide. However, the scriptures were written after the death of Jesus, and endured many revisions before becoming the Bible we know today. Gnostic philosophers and others made contributions to the early writings, but most of their documents were buried or destroyed. What we have today is a highly edited version of whatever Jesus might have said. And, although modern Christians believe suicide to be a mortal sin, some scholars maintain that no such proclamation exists in the Bible. In fact, biblical-studies scholar, Paul Middleton, argues that "many Jewish and Christian self-killings conform to Greco-Roman patterns [of] Noble Death."[27] That is, people willingly went to their deaths as an offering to God. Middleton claims that Judas did not commit suicide, but rather was "the victim of divine execution." He observes that early Christian martyrs demonstrated "not only enthusiasm for death, but suicide martyrdom."[28]

Suicide was, in fact, a common form of martyrdom until it was outlawed in the fourth century by St. Augustine, who observed large numbers of Christians dying as martyrs. He responded by declaring suicide a sin, thus laying the foundation for modern Christian thought on the subject.

From that time on, suicide seems to have carried a mostly singular and negative connotation among Christians. Christianity, however, could not erase the complexities of suicide, nor eliminate the human need to justify it under certain conditions. Centuries after the early philosophers, Sigmund Freud, in his

1920 essay *Beyond the Pleasure Principle*, attributed suicide to what he called the "death instinct," or *thanatos*. He believed that, in fact, "the aim of all life is death."[29] According to Freud, humankind has an innate capacity for self-destruction, equal to the drive to destroy others.

Interestingly, the Greek word *thanatos* was first used in a poem by Hesiod to describe the god of death, whose name was Thanatos, and who could be violent when ruled over by Keres or gentle when under the influence of Hypnos, Thanatos's twin brother. In the latter case, death is depicted as an angel. Freud himself committed a form of assisted suicide when he enlisted his physician to prescribe an overdose of morphine when the pain from cancer became too much for him to bear. Nevertheless, Freud believed that suicide often reflected anger turned inward. Rather than destroy the object of one's anger, an individual destroys himself, according to Freud.

In modern times, we see anger operating to destroy both others and oneself, as in cases of "murder by cop," in which an individual provokes the police into meting out death. Suicide may also follow a mass killing, and, in that way, share a similarity with the Mediterranean practice of devotio.

Forces outside oneself may also factor into many suicides. Certain locations even seem to invite suicide, among them the Golden Gate Bridge, as well as tall buildings, an ocean cliff known as the Gap in Australia, and both Beachy Head and Humber Bridge in England. What calls people to these destinations, or to any other place, is so confusing that we have no way of understanding or making sense of it. A psychological explanation for the large numbers of suicides in certain locales is that these "suicidal sites" carry a kind of archetypal pull; or, as one author said, they are infused with the "flesh of memory."[30]

Archetypal field theory, which parallels the thinking of French historian Pierre Nora and builds on C. G. Jung's theory of archetypes, contends that such "attractor sites" function as signs, symbols, and rituals with topological features that serve as a magnetic attraction for some people, and an aversion for others.

One location in Japan that is particularly known for suicide is the Aokigahara Forest, located northwest of the majestic Mount Fuji. It draws an estimated one hundred people a year to its sprawling 13.5 square miles of forest so thick with foliage that it is known as the Sea of Trees. To the Japanese, it is known as the Suicide Forest.[31] Although it attracts interested visitors, as well as well as suicides, it is no place for a leisurely stroll. The trees twist and turn, their roots winding along the forest floor in treacherous threads. The ground is uneven, rocky, and perforated with hundreds of caves, creating a feeling of profound isolation and stillness. One could indeed say that death seems close in such a place.

4

SUICIDE AND THE SOUL

It is impossible to speak of belief in spirits without at the same time considering the belief in souls. . . . [The soul's] essential characteristic is to be animated; it therefore represents the life *principle.*

—C. G. Jung

Although we have explored various attitudes about suicide, including Christianity's, there is another essential aspect in the discourse: the role of the soul. Although *soul* is considered a religious concept, the word appears as early as the eighth to sixth centuries BC in Homeric poems. According to the *Stanford Encyclopedia of Philosophy*, the poems depict the soul as "something that a human being risks in battle and loses in death. On the other hand, it is what at the time of death departs from the person's limbs and travels to the underworld, where it has a more or less pitiful afterlife as a shade or image of the deceased person."[1]

Thus, by the classical period in Greece (480–323 BC), philosophers were addressing the question of the soul, even before Christianity did. Socrates had perhaps the most cogent view: he claimed that the soul is not only immortal, but is capable of contemplating truths after its separation from the body at the time of death. He could not, however, make a convincing argument for the soul's immortality. Following him, Plato divided the soul into three components: reason, spirit, and appetite. He believed that the soul is the source of life, and the mind—that as a body dies, the soul is continually reborn, and able to think.[2]

The development of religion coincided with, and in some cases replaced, early Greek and Roman philosophy. Among the great religions that have emerged are Confucianism, Daoism, Sikhism, Shintoism, Islam, and several other ancient theologies. In the first century AD, Christianity took its place among the religious pantheon. Each religion had its own philosophy of life and death, and prescriptions for how to live in this life, as well as beliefs about the next one: that is, whether there is life after death, and, if so, what the nature of that life is, and what is needed to achieve it. Central to most religions is the idea of a soul as an entity that survives the body, whether such a thing exists or not.

Christianity adopted and expanded the concept of a soul as described by the early philosophers, forming a more cohesive idea of what the soul is, and of its role in the life–death–rebirth cycle. Christianity also determined what happens to the soul, based on certain conditions. The Ten Commandments are a general guide for immoral behavior, but Christianity pronounced additional behaviors as sins, too.

Eastern religions have their own ideas about life, death, and the hereafter. Like Christians, Hindus believe in a soul, which they call the *atman*. Viewing suicide to be a sin, they deem it to be a violation of *dharma*—the inherent nature of reality—and disobedience to the will of God. Suicide brings shame and disgrace upon the families, especially if committed by women. However, Hindus condone meritorious acts of self-sacrifice, which they call *atmahuti*, or *atmatyagam*.[3] Suicide in general signifies the murder of the soul, or Self. What determines whether one has committed such a sin is one's intention in performing the act: If the intention is to escape one's obligations to God and to others, it is considered suicide and brings consequences for the soul. But if the self-destruction is performed as the ultimate act of renunciation, it is seen as selfless, and an expression of love.

Such religious or spiritually motivated acts of suicide were more revered in ancient times. Today, self-immolation and starvation are common forms of protest against social or political ills. We witnessed this with the death of Buddhist monks during the Vietnam War.

Unlike Christianity, Hinduism does not believe that the souls of people who commit suicide go to hell immediately; rather, they wander the earth as "bad spirits" until the time when they were meant to die, at which time they are summoned to hell. Eventually, however, they are reborn afresh to continue their spiritual journey and complete their *karma*—meaning the sum of one's actions that determine one's fate.

Buddhism originated in India about the fifth century BCE, and eventually spread to the Far East, and around the world. Buddhists do not believe in a God as such, nor do they believe in the permanence of anything. In contrast to the *atman* (Self) of Hinduism, Buddhists refer to the *anatman*—the concept that there is no Self (or soul).[4] Buddhism does not address suicide specifically, but it implicitly prohibits it by forbidding killing, or violence of any kind, as the first principle of right behavior in what is known as the Sixteen Precepts, similar in substance to the Ten Commandments in Christianity.

Buddhists view life as a cycle of suffering and rebirth. Yet, if one strives to follow the Sixteen Precepts, and stops clinging to an illusory sense of self, one may eventually reach enlightenment (*nirvana*) and escape the cycle forever. The first to reach nirvana, according to the religion, was Siddhartha Gautama; hence he is known as the *Buddha* (*Skt.* Enlightened One.) Siddhartha achieved enlightenment in his own lifetime, but the concept of reincarnation seemingly offers everyone the chance to keep returning until enlightenment is achieved. If one returns reincarnated, however, it will not be as the "I" one knows oneself to be, although that may be what the ego wishes. The current "I" will not continue, perhaps even as a human being. It is best, therefore, to strive for enlightenment in the present lifetime. In this respect, nonkilling being the first precept of right behavior, committing suicide would clearly not help one escape the cycle of suffering.

Christians defer to the teachings of Christ, who suggested that those who followed him and his teachings would have everlasting life, making survival of the soul conditional. Essential to entry into heaven is the absence of sin. Since killing oneself is considered a sin—an act against God—people who commit suicide cannot go to heaven. Unlike the early philosophers who left the decision about life and death to the gods, Christians cannot ask God for permission to kill themselves.

The punishment for suicide, according to modern Christian doctrine, is sentencing to purgatory, or being sent directly to hell. In either case, the soul will suffer. There is little opportunity for redemption. Ironically, the Bible itself does not take a stand on suicide, despite the ubiquitous claims that it does. Instead, the holy book is littered with examples of people who did kill themselves, including Judas, Jesus's own disciple, who hanged himself in guilt for betraying his lord. As we have seen, this interpretation of Judas's behavior is disputed, but whether we call it suicide, or something else, his death was at his own hand.

Interestingly, the issue of soul has seen a resurgence in certain psychological circles, including those of Jungian psychology. The most prominent Jungian writer in this regard is James Hillman, who begins his book *Suicide and the Soul* by questioning the practice of suicide prevention, claiming that we should approach the suicide problem not from the viewpoints of society, or from the field of mental health, "but in relation to death and the soul."[5] He says that suicide is not only "an exit from life but also an entrance to death."[6] Hillman claims that while the soul cannot be accurately defined, nor truly understood from a scientific or medical perspective, it can be approached from the perspective of the individual psyche. Instead of a "concept," says Hillman, we might think of soul as a "symbol."[7] As he states:

> *"The soul is a deliberately ambiguous concept resisting all definition in the same manner as do all ultimate symbols that provide the root metaphors for the systems of human thought...*

What a person brings to the analytical hour are the sufferings of the soul; while the meanings discovered, the experiences shared, and the intentionality of the therapeutic process are all expressions of a living reality, which cannot be better apprehended than by the root metaphor of psychology, the psyche or soul."[8]

To understand suicide, Hillman proposes understanding the life of the suicidal individual, which also involves an enquiry into the unconscious of the individual and their deepest fantasies. "Because suicide is a way of entering death and because the problem of entering death releases the most profound fantasies of the human soul, to understand a suicide, we need to know what mythic fantasy is being created," says Hillman.[9]

At the same time, Hillman does not encourage people to commit suicide willy-nilly. In fact, voluntarily ending one's life is a most serious undertaking, and not to be taken lightly, nor necessarily alone. Echoing some of the early philosophers, Hillman claims that personal suffering is not enough to warrant killing oneself, and that individuals who are thinking of doing so must consider the needs and desires of the soul, not just the ego. In this way, Hillman might agree with Socrates, who died a conscious death, one chosen after careful, thoughtful consideration for the effect on both the individual and the world soul. Freud might also fall into this category, since he consulted his family before his assisted suicide. The key is to bring the impulse for death to consciousness so that it can be considered in the light of one's highest purpose.

5

JUNG AND SUICIDE

You ought to realize that suicide is murder, since after suicide there remains a corpse exactly as with any ordinary murder. Only it is yourself that has been killed.

—C. G. Jung

C. G. Jung was a protege of Sigmund Freud. Like Freud, Jung believed that human beings act not just on what is known consciously, but also on what is unknown, or unconscious, and thus hidden from our awareness. Jung called his theory "analytical psychology," in contrast to Freud's theory of psychoanalysis. Both approaches sought to bring the unconscious into consciousness. Both theories utilized dreams to do so, although they differed somewhat in terms of the symbolic meaning that they gave to the images that emerged in dreams. Freud's interpretations tended to be more reductive, or narrowly defined, while Jung's were more expansive. For example, Freud used the term *libido* to refer to sexual libido, while Jung interpreted *libido* as the life force, which can include sexual libido, but is not limited to that interpretation. Thus, if someone dreamed about a penis, Freud would say it was an image of sexuality, while Jung would say it was an image of the life-giving force. Both believed that individuals could benefit by tapping into messages from the unconscious through dreams. Making the unconscious conscious assists in self-discovery, and promotes the process of individuation, according to Jung.

Individuation is not about becoming a "good person"; it is about becoming one's unique self, equipped with all the potentials available to humankind, yet arranged in the unique patterns and colors that create an original personality. Akin to the concept of individuation, is the term *wholeness*. Jung said that the more individuated one is, the more whole he or she is. That's because wholeness involves developing all parts of oneself, all possibilities, not just the "nice" parts. For example, a person who identifies only with being loving, generous, and kind may sacrifice other qualities, such as assertiveness, honesty, and even self-reflection, that are needed to round out the personality. The individual may reject the latter qualities as "bad," and thus, push such qualities into the unconscious. The feared, or rejected, qualities in us, such as selfishness, or aggression, form what Jung called the Shadow, meaning characteristics the individual views as "bad." Analysis helps people to integrate these parts consciously into their personality.

Jung also talked about personality types, such as introversion and extraversion, and how a person can become too one-sided in their development. An extravert may never develop his or her introverted qualities, nor an introvert the extraverted qualities. We come into the world with both traits, but have an inherent tendency toward one or the other. These form one pair of opposites. We also have a proclivity toward a dominant function in two more pairs of opposites: thinking/feeling and intuition/sensation. Just as with introversion and extraversion, we each have all four of these functions but tend to favor one over the others. Thinking and feeling determine how we make judgments about things; intuition and sensation determine how we take in what we perceive. We usually develop one function of each pair, while the other functions get neglected, at least initially. The more-developed functions are considered our strengths—or superior functions; they enable us to become successful at tasks and in careers requiring those strengths. The less-developed functions atrophy if we don't eventually develop them as well, which is usually done later in life. These "inferior functions" become like muscles that we rarely use. Wholeness—individuation—requires that we develop all four functions: thinking/feeling and intuition/sensation, as well as introversion/extraversion. If not, we can become rigidly one-sided. This one-sidedness may cause problems as we age, and may give rise to depression, phobias, and other forms of neuroses.

As a child, I developed, or tried to develop, the functions my family valued, including extraversion, thinking, and sensation. What was more natural to me—my intuition, feeling, and introversion, was not valued; those functions flowered only when I was older, and able to fully embrace my true self after much psychological work.

In Jung's theory of personality and individuation, he focused more on living than dying, but he was also intimately concerned with issues of the soul, at times speculating about what happens after death. In 1955, he is quoted as telling a terminally ill individual, "I have good reasons to assume that things are not finished with death. Life seems to be an interlude in a long story."[1] Here, Jung seems to suggest that perhaps individuation continues even beyond death. Mostly, however, he concerns himself with development of the soul in this lifetime. Anything that cuts short this life, such as suicide, reduces the chances for individuation before death. This seems to be the message he conveyed to a young female client who attempted suicide when she was twenty-one. Jung told her, "It isn't possible to kill part of your 'self.' If you ruin your conscious personality, the so-called ego-personality, you deprive the Self of its real goal."[2] In Jung's mind, the goal of life is the realization of the Self.

Jung made rather scant mention of suicide in the numerous volumes of his collected works. What he does say, is that suicide is the result of the ego being overwhelmed by unconscious contents—that is, by forces larger than the ego. As we know, the ego resides in the conscious part of the psyche. The unconscious includes both suppressed, and never-known, contents. It also includes both personal, and collective, contents. Together, they form a Self, which Jung believed to be the central organizing principle of the psyche. When a person commits suicide, they not only end the life of their body, they also cut short the development of the Self.

In a letter he sent in 1946, Jung writes:

> The idea of suicide, understandable as it is, does not seem commendable to me. We live in order to gain the greatest possible amount of spiritual development and self-awareness. As long as life is possible, even if only in a minimal degree, you should hang onto it, in order to scoop it up for the

purpose of conscious development. To interrupt life before its time is to bring to a standstill an experiment which we have not set up. We have found ourselves in the midst of it and must carry it through to the end.[3]

This perspective might echo the philosophies of the early Greeks, but to Jung, it is not to please the gods or society that one must see things through to the end; it is because the soul demands it. Corresponding with Elanor Bertine in 1946 regarding the death of Kristine Mann, a cofounder of the Analytical Psychology Club of New York, Jung seems to have changed course. Mann, a devotee of analytical psychology, and of Jung, had committed suicide after a long illness. It is said that a few months before her death, and while experiencing much pain and depression, she experienced an ineffable light glowing in her hospital room. This mysterious light lasted for more than an hour, and was followed by a deep sense of peace and joy. Her mind deteriorated after that experience, but the memory remained. Jung believed that the moment she saw the light, her spirit left her body, and she was able to ease into death. Regarding her passing, he said:

> It is really a question whether a person affected by such a terrible illness should or may end her life. It is my attitude in such cases not to interfere. . . . I'm convinced that if anybody has it in himself to commit suicide, then practically the whole of his being is going that way. . . . I think nothing is really gained by interfering with such an issue. It is presumably to be left to the free choice of the individual.[4]

So, on the one hand, Jung thinks it ill advised to hurry along the process of death, and on the other, he seems to accept that doing so is perhaps what the soul, or the Self, wishes, at least in certain cases. In my mind, Jung seems to agree with both Socrates and Plato. Jung suggests that the Self is somehow involved in the decision to end one's life, and that therefore we must withhold judgment to some degree, as Plato might have said. At the same time, Jung has replaced "God" and "the gods" with the "Self" in a way with which Socrates might have agreed.

In that same correspondence, Jung says:

> If Kristine Mann had committed suicide under the stress of unbearable pain, I should have thought that this was the right thing. As it was not the case, I think it was in her stars to undergo such a cruel agony for reasons that escape our understanding. Our life is not made entirely by ourselves. The main bulk of it is brought into existence out of sources that are hidden to us. Even complexes can start a century or more before a man is born. There is something like karma.[5]

Here, Jung almost seems to invoke Buddhist thinking, but ultimately his message suggests that we remain open to the mysteries of life and death.

In later years, Jung may have given more thought to the issue of suicide. He continued to struggle with the idea that one must see the development of the Self through to the end, but he began to speculate on what could happen to make a person take his or her own life. He talks about the power of the unconscious, which, as mentioned earlier, can overwhelm the personality and lead to a nervous breakdown. According to Jung:

> This [the breakdown] invariably happens when the influence of the unconscious finally paralyzes all conscious action. The demands of the unconscious then . . . bring about a disastrous split which shows itself in one of two ways: either the subject no longer knows what he really wants, and nothing interests him, or he wants too much at once and has too many interests, but in impossible things. . . . In more extreme cases the split ends in suicide.[6]

To Jung, then, suicidal tendencies stem from inner conflicts that paralyze the ability of the ego to adapt. This occurs when there is not enough ego development to contend with the powerful effects of unconscious material. Says Jung:

> We are greatly mistaken if we think that the unconscious is something harmless that could be made into an object of entertainment, a parlor game. Certainly, the unconscious is not always, and in all circumstances, dangerous, but as soon as a neurosis is present it is a sign of a special heaping up of energy in the unconscious, like a charge that may explode. Here, caution is indicated.[7]

Jung seems to be warning us of digging around in the unconscious too deeply, even in the service of individuation, as when someone enters analysis. As he says, "One never knows what one may be releasing when one begins to analyze dreams. Something deeply buried and invisible may thereby be set in motion. . . . When neurotic symptoms are present one must proceed very carefully." According to Jung, analysis itself "activates the unconscious," so that it breaks through in ways that may lead to a mental disorder, "and possibly even suicide."[8]

There is something almost fatalistic in Jung's appreciation, and respect, for the power of unconscious forces, underscoring his belief in its ultimate effect on the lives of human beings. As he states elsewhere:

> Although in the great majority of cases compensation aims at establishing a normal psychological balance and thus appears as a kind of self-regulation of the psychic system, one must not forget that under certain circumstances and in certain cases (for instance, in the latent psychoses) compensation may lead to a fatal outcome owing to the preponderance of destructive tendencies. The result [is] suicide or some other abnormal action, apparently preordained in the life-pattern of certain hereditarily tainted individuals.[9]

Jung thus believed that the analytic process itself could unleash a preexisting psychosis, something for the savvy analyst to bear in mind. While he believed that most mental illnesses arise from a disintegration of consciousness caused by invasion of unconscious contents, he continued to hold hope for people to override this terrible fate. Says Jung:

> I have also seen patients who . . . sometimes developed a suicidal tendency but, because of their inherent reasonableness, prevented it from becoming conscious and in this way generated an unconscious suicide-complex. This unconscious urge to suicide then engineered all kinds of dangerous accidents. . . . When it was possible to make the suicidal leaning conscious in these cases, common sense could intervene as a salutary check: the patients could then consciously recognize and avoid the situations that tempted them to self-destruction.[10]

Here, Jung seems to understand the complexities of suicidal ideation and actual suicide. He appreciates the benefit of certain defense systems that serve to hold back unconscious material that could be dangerous to the individual if made conscious. He also understands that, under some circumstances, intervention may derail what could be one's fate. This may explain my own fate. If, in fact, my "weaker nature" led me to develop a "suicide complex," then my attempt at suicide made me conscious of it. Thereafter, I could consciously recognize its existence, and avoid situations that tempted me toward self-destruction. I did so by developing a psychological perspective that weakened the destructive pull, while giving its existence meaning and purpose. Without that intervention, my attempt could have gone awry, in which case I would not have lived to discover the meaning in it.

Whether Jung would say it was my destiny—or the will of the Self—that I lived is unclear.

Despite Jung's awareness, and even compassion, for individuals who are overcome by the archetypal forces, he finally cannot condone suicide. Given his conviction that the Self is what directs us through life, and that one's life purpose is precisely the realization of this Self, suicide seems the ultimate abdication. Hence, he says simply, "Suicide is murder, since after suicide there remains a corpse exactly as with any ordinary murder. Only it is yourself that has been killed."[11]

One wonders, though, how Jung felt about Freud's suicide, in that it was not a case of interrupted development or invasion of unconscious contents. It was a conscious decision, propelled by inescapable physical pain. Freud's death was truly an assisted suicide. Would Jung have conceptualized such a death differently than he would have one driven by mental illness—in other words, by emotional, not physical, pain? Did he even consider other kinds of suicides, as he seemed to do in the case of Kristine Mann? Did he consider, for example, the suicide of Socrates?

What we do know, is that Jung made a case for protecting the individuation process against unconscious forces that might lead us down the road to suicide. As long as one lives, the individuation process continues. After that, we do not know. Nor do we know if suicide is ever part and parcel of the individuation process. Dr. Kaye Gersch, a psychoanalyst in South Wales, maintains that "as a Jungian, I uphold the position that Individuation is the fundamental calling and responsibility in life and in our time, although I acknowledge that each person fulfils the individuation imperative in different degrees and sometimes not at all."[12]

6

MODERN VIEWS OF SUICIDE

Anything that seems wrong to us can be right under certain circumstances over which we have no control and the end of which we do not understand.
—C. G. Jung

The contemporary view of suicide, which originated in the nineteenth century, is more psychological than philosophical in its approach. Psychology is a relatively new science that was founded by Wilhelm Wundt in Germany and William James in America, both of whom are credited for creating a new academic and scientific field distinct from philosophy. In 1879, Wundt opened a laboratory in Germany for the study of feelings and sensations, while James published the first major textbook, *The Principles of Psychology*, in America in the late 1800s.

Psychology is the study of behavior, although depth psychology—often called *analytical psychology* or *psychoanalysis*—concerns itself with the psyche, and thus, the unconscious. Social psychology, the study of behavior in a social context, and behavioral psychology, as well as neuroscience, which is concerned with the brain, were all developed later, as were various other offshoots of psychological theory. Not all of them focused on suicide, but their ideas informed the theories that did.

Today, we often lump the various psychological disciplines under the heading "mental-health professionals." Psychologists, marriage and family therapists, psychiatric social workers, and other kinds of mental-health workers are tasked with diagnosing and treating people with mental-health problems. They are concerned not only with suicide, but with *suicidality*—that is, with the thoughts, feelings, and actions taken by a person wanting to die. They view suicide in stages, running the gamut from suicidal ideation (thinking about killing oneself or wanting to die) to completed suicide. In practice, however, therapists are more familiar with the least lethal of these: suicidal ideation, and they are constantly assessing for it in depressed and mentally ill clients. To determine the seriousness of the threat, therapists ask the following questions: Does the client have thoughts of killing himself? Does he or she have a plan for how to commit suicide? And, finally, does he or she possess the means necessary to carry out the act of suicide? If the answer to all three is yes, steps may be taken to intervene and protect him from following through on his or her plan.

Most of the time, however, clients report only one of the three answers used to determine the seriousness of the threat: thoughts of killing themselves, and these thoughts may be as mild as wishing they weren't here or that they want to "end things." This was the wordage Meghan Markle used on *The Oprah Winfrey Show*, when she and husband, U.K.'s Prince Harry, were interviewed about Meghan's experience of adjusting to life in a royal family. After admitting her suicidal thoughts, Markle was accused in the media of trying to get attention. This is a common attitude toward celebrities who contemplate suicide, as if the outward trappings of wealth and success should inoculate such individuals against such thoughts.

Yet, the rich and famous are no more immune to thoughts about suicide than anyone else. Not only do they think about it, but many act on it, and when they do so, we are horrified—as happened when celebrities Anthony Bourdain, Robin Williams, and Freddie Prinze killed themselves. It's as if we want to believe that if things are going well on the outside (particularly as regards fame and wealth), the inside must also be in good shape. The truth is that we all walk a precarious tightrope between life and death. As Freud said, "The aim of life is death."[1]

Throughout history, humankind has been called to answer the question posed by Shakespeare's Hamlet, "To be or not to be." When a person believes that "being" is a choice, he feels freed of the power that death holds over him. Psychiatrist, Thomas Szasz, quotes Wolfgang von Goethe as saying that "suicide is an event that is part of human nature. Regardless of what has been said and done about it in the past, every person must confront that same question for himself anew, and every age must come to its own terms with it." Szasz goes on to write: Behind Goethe's simple statement lies a profound truth: dying voluntarily is a choice intrinsic to human existence. It is our ultimate, fatal freedom[2] That said, let's look at the development of a psychological view of suicide.

Suicide and Mental Illness

As a field of study, psychology is interested in the *why* of suicide. The idea, first posited by Sigmund Freud, was that suicide is caused by mental illness. Freud, and others of his time, postulated that individuals could suffer from mental, as well as from physical, illness. Psychology sought to understand and heal mental illness. Doing so changed how people viewed killing themselves. No longer was suicide considered just a philosophical matter of "to be or not to be." Nor was it simply a sin against God. Instead, suicide was viewed as the consequence of an illness of the mind. Now, the individual choosing suicide over other options would be viewed as suffering from some kind of psychological problem that clouded their judgment, and from which they needed to be cured.

Theories about how to treat suicidal people mushroomed in the years after Freud. Psychiatrists, psychologists, sociologists, neurologists, and others offered their views on the subject, positing their own theories about the cause and treatment of mental illness and suicidality.

In the mid-twentieth century, the American Psychiatric Association compiled a list of mental disorders that they outlined in a book called *The Diagnostic and Statistical Manual* (DSM), which today serves as a bible for mental health professionals. The DSM was the brainchild of psychiatrists, mostly men, who were esteemed physicians, and were thus given authority to define aberrant behavior in medical terms. While the DSM does not define suicidality per se as a mental disorder, the field of psychiatry and psychology claim a connection between the psychiatric disorders the DSM describes and the act of suicide.

In other words, people with certain disorders are more likely to commit suicide than people without these disorders, according to mental-health professionals.

Unfortunately, this way of thinking has led to a cause-and-effect association between mental illness and suicide, an idea that has proved detrimental to many mentally ill persons who are not suicidal.

Research on the relationship between suicide and mental illness has been mixed. In the 1900s, studies claimed that as many as 90 percent of people who killed themselves were mentally ill.[3] Those numbers, however, were biased by the techniques used to determine them.[4] Early statistics on suicide and mental illness were based largely on people who were diagnosed after the fact, often using a "psychological autopsy," which is a diagnostic tool involving detailed reports from family members, friends, and others who might have been able to comment on the person's mental condition at the time of death. Such reports were thus skewed by those who described the deceased person's symptoms.[5]

Since the early 1900s, studies have been conducted on suicides among people suffering from specific illnesses, such as depression, schizophrenia, and other mental illnesses, who were diagnosed prior to killing themselves. These studies, including one in 2008, indicate high rates of suicide among this population.[6] But while the studies focused on patients with a diagnosable illness, they were limited to people in mental hospitals, so they did not account for the many depressed and bipolar individuals seeking outpatient treatment for situation-specific depression, not to mention the people who do not seek treatment at all.

Currently, it is estimated that about half the people who commit suicide have suffered from a mental condition.[7] One study estimates the risk of suicide to be as low as 5 to 8 percent for people diagnosed with disorders such as depression, alcoholism, and schizophrenia. The authors of the study say that suicide is more "multi-factorial" than simply mental-illness based. Ethnicity, adverse childhood experiences, and other factors play a large role.[8]

Nevertheless, the general thinking has been that people with certain diagnoses are inherently at high risk for suicide. While this may be true for some people with severe and chronic mental illness who have been hospitalized, it is not true of mentally ill people in general. According to a CDC report in 2019, 54 percent of people who commit suicide have no known mental illness.[9]

Individuals who are not mentally ill at the time of suicide may be suffering from more everyday issues such as relationship or job problems, financial struggles, or even substance abuse. A review of the literature shows that the risk of suicide increases when substances are added to an already toxic mix of other contributing factors.

That is not to say, of course, that a person who is severely depressed won't commit suicide. Many of them do. After their death, others who knew them often give mental illness as the reason for their action. "That's why he killed himself," people will say. "He was depressed." But that conclusion is overly simplistic. Several factors must converge before a depressed person takes his or her life. Among them are the complete loss of hope that things will get better, the belief that dying will lift the burden of one's chronic bad feelings, or will save or enhance the life of another, or the belief that it will achieve any number of other goals the person has set up for him- or herself. The specific combination of factors is always uniquely individual, although some of the contributing factors may be similar across cases.

My brother, for example, was depressed, alcoholic, and showed all of the symptoms of ADHD—all DSM diagnoses that, in his case, were long term. However, he also suffered from chronic shame, intense rage, financial ruin, social isolation, and a complete loss of hope. From the note he left behind, it seems that he also wanted what resources he had left given to his son. In that way, he could redeem himself in death. In addition, he had all the three preconditions for suicide: ideation, a plan, and the means. For him, it was a matter of choosing the right time. It's as if everything in his life culminated in a perfect storm of feelings, thoughts, and events that led inevitably to his death.

In my own case, I was diagnosed with situational depression after the fact, but shame, hopelessness, poor self-esteem, financial and career collapse, and relationship loss exacerbated what might have otherwise been a mild to moderate depression. Some might also call it grief. The depression was the result of all the other conditions. I was in crisis, a time when suicide intervention is most crucial and successful.

Suicide as a Mental-Health Issue

As discussed, decisions about suicide in ancient times were determined by the state, as with the Romans, who established codes and laws governing which people, and why, they could kill themselves. Suicide was later considered a sin by Christianity and other religions. Calling it a sin held accountable the person who committed the act. It made suicide a moral issue. The advent of psychology changed suicide from a moral to a mental-health issue, thus removing responsibility and morality from the equation. The mental-illness approach says that suicidal people are not to blame as they are sick; their mental illness is directing their behavior. And, remedies for said mental illnesses range from herbal remedies and potions to antidepressants and antipsychotic medications.

This approach has advantages and disadvantages. Attributing the death to a disease makes it more palpable to those left behind, for then they know it was out of the person's control. At the same time, the attribution of death to disease might oversimplify what the now-deceased person was struggling with, and so obscure, or minimize, the depth of meaning of the suicidal act. Survivors might feel better with the "disease" label, but it could be a disservice to the person who died.

This is certainly the view of many professionals. James Hillman, and Thomas Szasz, who was a champion of individual rights, as well as a psychiatrist, agreed that to want to kill oneself is not a disease. Furthermore, they agreed that suicide cannot be adequately understood, or addressed, from a strictly medical perspective. Dr. Szasz claimed that dying voluntarily is "our ultimate, fatal freedom," and he suggested that perhaps the time is ripe for rethinking our attitude about suicide, and its relation to the medical profession. "To accomplish this," he said that "we must de-medicalize and destigmatize voluntary death and accept it as a behavior that has always been and will always be a part of the human condition." He noted that "wanting to die or killing oneself is sometimes blameworthy, sometimes praiseworthy, and sometimes neither; it is not a disease; it cannot be a bona fide medical treatment; and it can never justify deprivation of liberty."[10]

Dr. Kaye Gersch would agree, insisting that there is a common misconception that only people diagnosed as mentally ill would consider suicide. "There are indications that suicidal thoughts and impulses are fundamental and an almost universal experience of being human," she says. Moreover, she points out that most people resolve suicidal thoughts and impulses without committing suicide.[11]

Gersch believes that suicidal ideation can stem variously from major life events; an existential situation (meaning intrinsic to existence); altruistic intentions, such as "death before dishonor"; the desire to make a sacrifice for political or religious reasons; the will to martyrdom, often in the service of a religious ideology; and disappointed love, as in Wagner's opera *Tristan and Isolde*. Even the compulsion to be part of a group suicide (as in cults or social pacts) can play a role. Gersch notes that, in such instances, ". . . the person has become less important than the group, and we could see this as an abdication of the individuation process. As a Jungian, I uphold the position that individuation is the fundamental calling and responsibility in life and in our time, although I acknowledge that each person fulfils the individuation imperative in different degrees and sometimes not at all."[12]

I hold a similar position to want to take the "sick" out of suicide and replace it with an understanding of the complex reasons of why people kill themselves. Rather than ask why people commit suicide, I prefer to ask why "this particular person" at "this particular time" and in "this particular way" decided to exit his or her life and what he or she hoped to find on the other side.

Dr. Gersch points out that James Hillman builds on the Hippocratic principle of "First, do no harm" by adding the word *soul*: "First, do no harm to the soul." Gersch agrees with Hillman, stating that "the perspective of the soul informs us about our obligation to life itself."[13] Although the point of view of the soul is an essential ingredient in deciding about whether "to be or not to be," I do not believe that I, or anyone else, can adequately make the determination for someone else. It is my role, as an analyst, to address and explore the issue with my client, and to discuss the possible consequences of whatever decision they make. In my view, perhaps contrary to Gersch's, suicide might well be a part of a person's individuation journey.

Thomas Joiner, in his book *Why People Die by Suicide*, tells of a man who spent most of his life in mental institutions who said, "If I commit suicide, it will not be to destroy myself but to put myself back together again. Suicide will be for me only one means of violently reconquering myself."[14] In a sense, the man was essentially seeking transformation, and could not seem to find a way in this life. Who is to say if he was right or wrong?

The Medicalization of Suffering

The medicalization of psychological suffering began around the turn of the twentieth century. The primary pioneer in this field was Sigmund Freud, who departed from his religious and philosophical predecessors by introducing the role of the unconscious in the manifestation of maladaptive behavior, including suicide. Although Freud did not initially weigh in on the subject at the 1910 Vienna Psychoanalytic Society, where the subject of adolescent suicide emerged, he later recognized suicide as a manifestation of the death instinct.

Freud was among the psychological thinkers of his time who theorized that suicide was an attempt to regain a lost object that was both loved and hated.[15] In essence, suicide, according to Freud, expresses a repressed wish to kill an ambivalently regarded lost love object, and thus, is ultimately an act of revenge, suggesting that anger is part of the equation. Freud thought that when one is depressed, the hatred that is felt toward the object is internalized, and becomes identified with the "self," which can then be destroyed. This is the meaning of the concept of anger turned inward. In his thinking, the depressed patient is melancholic in response to an inability to adequately grieve the loss of a loved person, or who the patient has idealized that person to be. Freud associated this kind of melancholy with narcissism, or a deep and intense self-absorption.

I remember my psychiatrist asking me, after my suicide attempt, if I felt any anger toward Josh, the man who lived with me in Boston, and then left me in California—the last loss I endured before attempting suicide. At the time, I said no. I felt humiliation and a deep sense of grief. Later, in analysis, I realized the anger went further back than either Josh or my ex-husband. It went back to my parents: rejection by my father, and shame by my mother. Mostly, I was angry at them for fostering so little self-esteem in me that I could not develop a healthy ego, and thus, no relationship with the Self. In his early work, Freud seems to suggest that in cases where the superego becomes too harsh in its attack on the ego, the ego is abandoned and left to die. This is what happened to me as a result of the assaults on my fragile ego from an early age. I began punishing myself for being such an unlovable human being. Only later, as I developed a healthier ego, did I access my anger.

My brother, too, carried much anger, mostly at the family. Perhaps, that is because the family mirrored a negative view of him that he himself held unconsciously. It was as if there were mirrors everywhere, showing him his own self-hatred—that would be enough to make anyone angry, or depressed, or shamed. I believe he experienced all three.

When Freud planned his own death, anger had nothing to do with it. He stated, "I have one wholly secret entreaty: no invalidism, no paralysis of one's powers through bodily misery. Let us die in harness, as King Macbeth says."[16] Thus, when the pain from his illness became too much for him, he turned to his physician, Max Schur, imploring, "Schur, you remember our contract not to leave me in the lurch when the time had come. Now it is nothing but torture and makes no sense. Talk it over with Anna [Freud's daughter], and if she thinks it's right, then make an end of it."[17] In Freud's case, it was physical, not mental, illness that motivated his decision to die.

Herbert Hendin, Professor of Psychiatry at NYU Medical College, and Medical Director of Suicide Prevention Initiatives, claims that most mentally-ill patients are not suicidal, and he differentiates those who are, from those who are not. The differentiating factor is the person's affective state. Among the emotional states that indicate high risk for suicide are rage, hopelessness, despair, desperation, and guilt. He also suggests several ways that people make meaning out of their self-inflicted death. For some, there is hope of reunion with some lost object. In this case, the desire is not to escape something in this life, but to move toward something in the next life.[18]

Psychologist Bruno Klopfer, who studied with Jung, lists six situations in which death seems preferable to life, whether the reason is rational, or not. Regarding reunion with a lost object, Klopfer says, "Reunion with a dead loved one is sought in cases where the death of a loved one seems to carry with it all the meaning of life. The desire to reunite with this person in death becomes so overwhelming that it does not even matter whether the individual has any concrete notion of how this reunion will take place."[19]

Literature is replete with examples of suicidal attempts to join a lost love, be that of a parent, child, or lover. Romeo and Juliet, Antony and Cleopatra, and Antigone are a few examples. Such stories reflect a common human desire for reunion with a beloved after death, and a willingness to kill oneself to achieve it. Although Greek and Shakespearean dramas can be violent and bloody, the motive of revenge in suicide is less clear, as with Hamlet's Ophelia, and with Lady MacBeth. Nevertheless, an exploration of revenge themes in clinical cases is well known.

While I was not conscious of any rage at the time of my suicide attempt, feelings of helplessness, despair, and desperation were fiercely coursing through my veins. I did not even feel guilt, despite my Christian upbringing. I did, however, feel shame. Sadly, I did not imagine a rebirth or reunion, at least not consciously. I imagined only a cessation of psychic suffering. Like other suicidal individuals with whom I have worked, I had no forward vision of life. It was completely black.

The Bible says, "Where there is no vision, the people perish" (Proverbs 29:18).[20] That proverb resonated with me when I first heard it as a stand-alone quote. However, the pronouncement is followed by, ". . . but he that keepeth the law, happy is he" (ibid.). The assumption is that this is God's vision and God's law, and the biblical author lists all the transgressions one could be culpable of—including lying, cheating, and other forms of wickedness, suggesting that punishment, rather than liberation, follows for those with no vision. The first part of the quote ("Where there is no vision, people perish") puts me in mind of hopelessness without meaning. The latter part of the quote (". . . he that keepeth the law, happy is he") might have more meaning if it were meant metaphorically, in which case I would interpret it to mean a higher law—that which gives life purpose.

Thomas Joiner agrees that mental illness alone does not make someone suicidal, but other factors, such as burdensomeness, and a failed sense of belonging, are key. According to Joiner, only a small minority of cases of psychological pain result in suicide. He insists that every case of suicide stems from excessive *psychache*,[21] when he quotes Edwin Shneidman, who first coined the term: "psychache" in his book, *The Suicidal Mind*.[22] Associating the term with the critical feelings of burdensomeness and failed belonging, Joiner suggests that the pain of psychache is "necessary but not sufficient for suicide."[23] He chooses to focus on the interrelationships of people, and how the inability to form meaningful relationships makes life unbearable. I tend to agree. As we become more and more alienated from our fellow beings, and from ourselves, we may risk experiencing the consequences associated with the feeling of a lack of belonging. According to Joiner, "Serious suicidal behavior requires the desire for death."[24] This desire stems from the frustration of basic needs, among them the need to belong, or connect to others, and to feel effective in influencing others. He observes that "two psychological conditions are necessary to the will to live, effectiveness and connectedness."[25] He further asserts that the literature on failed belongingness shows a connection between a failed sense of belonging and suicidal feelings.[26]

Joiner says that when all of these needs are snuffed out, suicide becomes attractive, but not accessible without the ability for self-harm. He believes that the ability to inflict harm may be the distinguishing factor between those who do, and those who do not commit suicide. He goes on to assert that the more times people attempt suicide, or get close to committing it, the more likely they are of eventually succeeding.[27] While this may be the case for serial suicide attempts, it is not true of everyone who attempts suicide. More often, and especially with therapeutic help, individuals who attempt suicide once, do not attempt it again. Where genetic or neurological factors are involved, however, individuals who attempt suicide and fail may, in fact attempt it multiple times, each time in a more lethal way, as Joiner suggests. I discuss this issue more in appendix C.

Meanwhile, Edwin Shneidman, who predated Joiner, would agree that psychological pain (psychache) is the basic ingredient in suicide.[28] However, he used the term *perturbation*, or felt pain, to describe the motivation for suicide. "By itself, mental anguish is not lethal," says Shneidman, "but lethality, when coupled with perturbation, is a principal ingredient in self-inflicted death."[29]

Shneidman separates felt pain, or perturbation, from lethality—the idea of death as the solution. "We can reduce the lethality if we lessen the anguish, the perturbation," he says.[30] But he does not support the idea of addressing lethality directly. Rather, "We can address thoughts about suicide by working with this person and asking why mental turmoil is leading to feelings of lethality."[31]

I tend to agree with Shneidman. In my experience, the anguish from which one is suffering is itself what is lethal. Too many suicide-prevention approaches are geared toward eliminating the means of lethality, instead of addressing the core issue of anguish, as I discovered both in working with a suicidal client of mine, and in my experience with my brother, Jimmy. Initially, Jimmy had bought a gun, the most lethal form of suicide; however, he ended up killing himself with something seemingly less lethal, probably drugs, because he did not address his own anguish.

Shneidman seems to view suicide as a tragic drama played out in one's mind. "It is intrinsically psychological—the pain of excessively felt shame, guilt, fear, anxiety, loneliness, angst, dread of growing old or dying badly," he says, adding that ". . . everyone who commits suicide feels driven by it—indeed feels that suicide is the only option left."[32] Again, I tend to agree. Suicide is a drive, perhaps a basic drive, but it is activated only under desperate conditions. It must be noted that Shneidman does not mention depression in his list of excessively felt forms of pain.

Much of Shneidman's research involved culling through forty years of suicide notes filed away in the Los Angeles County Coroner's Office, where he began his career as a suicidologist.

The results of his work filled the pages of several books in addition to *The Suicidal Mind*, which includes a psychological pain survey in the appendix. It also includes a listing of Henry Murray's psychogenic needs, positing the most important psychological needs experienced by human beings. He offers examples of some of the most prominent people in history who have committed suicide, and their reasons for doing so. The frustrated need for achievement and dominance came up most often. Ten out of twelve people rated the need for achievement as important, while five out of twelve rated a desire for dominance highly. The weight a person gives to each of these needs and their experience meeting them, says Shneidman, indicates either a high, or a low, level of mental anguish.

In recent years, the mental-health profession has partnered with neuroscientists to explore how the brain impacts our psychology, and vice versa, as I explore later in the book. One day, we may discover that suicidality is even more complex than we thought, incorporating a tapestry of physical, psychological, and spiritual elements, all interacting—body, mind, and spirit.

7
SUICIDE AND SHAME

I define shame as the intensely painful feeling or experience of believing that we are flawed and therefore unworthy of love and belonging.
—Brené Brown

Although the field of psychology acknowledges the role of shame in contributing to suicidal behavior, no one has made a direct link between the two until recently. That's because shame is not listed in the DSM, and is therefore not considered a mental illness by itself. Yet, shame can lead to depression, which the DSM does recognize as a mental illness, and depression can lead to suicide. The link between shame and suicidal behavior may be indirect, but it exists.

My purpose here is to single out the role of shame, and elevate its importance as a direct factor in suicidality, independent of depression. Over the past few decades, since my own brush with suicide, I wondered what factors drove me to want to kill myself. Clearly, I was depressed, but I wasn't necessarily suicidal, at least not initially. The immediate source of my depression was grief, hopelessness, and humiliation, although underneath was an intense shame—the kind of shame that I have witnessed in many of my clients who express suicidal thoughts.

Emile Durkheim, the quintessential French sociologist of the past century, was one of the first to talk about shame independent of any other diagnosis. He claimed that capitalism was to blame for a deep sense of shame in people who could not rise out of poverty. Thus, shame was an inner experience based on an outer situation. Since then, psychology has explored the relationships among poverty, shame, and depression. The research has shown that outer experiences, such as poverty and financial ruin, can indeed activate feelings of shame, as can exclusion from society due to religion, gender identity, and other social factors. But shame due to external factors is not the only kind of shame. Shame is ultimately an inner experience that can be painful, even paralyzing, regardless of its source.

Mario Jacoby, in *Shame and the Origins of Self-Esteem*, describes shame this way, "Shame makes us want to sink through the floor, crawl into a hole and die. And then we are really alone."[1]

The Greeks had a goddess of Shame, named Adios, who was a handmaiden of the greater goddess, Athena. Adios appeared during times of war, when shaming strategies were employed to motivate men to volunteer to fight, lest they be isolated from the collective, and figuratively shamed to death.

Robert Willie, in a 2014 paper for the Symposium of Dutch Psychoanalysts, describes a specific kind of shame that is often referred to as "toxic shame." I prefer the term "suicidal shame" because it involves "the shame of existing." Willie refers to the ". . . shame about existing as we are, and especially at the fact that we are."[2] Such shame constitutes a total rejection of the self and ". . . feelings of extreme worthlessness and inferiority, coupled with the all-pervasive conviction that it would be better not to exist."[3] This is the kind of shame I experienced when I became suicidal. That is not to say, I hadn't felt shame before then. In fact, my shame had been long standing, but it had never risen to the heights that I experienced during my suicidal phase—I felt shame about my very existence, and believed that I would be better off dead. That is suicidal shame.

Deep shame generally begins very early in life, often at the hands of primary caregivers, and then reinforced by the outer world. It is not situational. Shaming remarks, and attitudes toward a child's efforts to act independently, take risks, separate from parents, or disagree with them are foundational to the development of early shame. The absence of emotionally nurturing responses such as warmth, empathy, forgiveness, and compassion are also internalized in the shamed child in such a way that the child is unable to feel those emotions toward him- or herself. The child may even interpret the lack, or scarcity, of physical and emotional holding, or touching, as a form of rejection. That, too, is internalized. The combination of shaming remarks, and the absence of positive remarks, can lead to the kind of toxic, or suicidal shame, that Willie described.

Patricia A. DeYoung, a relational therapist, and author of *Understanding and Treating Chronic Shame*, says chronic shame is painful, corrosive, and elusive, which may even resist self-help, and undermine intensive psychoanalysis. DeYoung says that chronic shame, as opposed to shaming moments, can become wired into the brain, and become part of the personality.[4]

The Neurobiology of Shame

Like all strong affects, shame creates reactions in the brain, specifically in the amygdala. The amygdala plays an important role in arousal processing, as evidenced by neuroimaging studies that reveal a clear association between amygdala activation and shame induction.[5] One study noted how "shame plays a fundamental role in the regulation of our social behavior," and its authors suggest that the role of the amygdala in processing shame "might reflect its relevance in resolving ambiguity and uncertainty, in order to correctly detect social violations and to generate shame feelings."[6] Another study found evidence that "shame is associated with higher activations in regions linked to sensory perception of emotionally relevant stimuli."[7] The authors of this study go on to say, "This supports the hypothesis that shame and guilt play at least partly distinct roles in vulnerability to major depressive disorder. Shame-induction may be a more sensitive probe of residual amygdala hypersensitivity in major depressive disorder compared with facial emotion-evoked responses previously found to normalize remission."[8]

The same part of the brain associated with shame is also responsible for the well-known fight-or-flight response. This explains why acute shame often triggers fear, and provokes a need to hide or escape. John Kalafat and David Lester report one researcher as saying, "When we experience shame, then our desire is to hide, to withdraw from the situation, to fall through the floor."[9] Interestingly, the word *shame* comes from an old English word meaning "to hide." Kalafat and Lester underscore the relationship between fear and shame. As they explain, fear of facing those who know of our unworthiness may, under some conditions, lead to "the ultimate withdrawal—suicide."[10] Individuals suffering from deep shame often fear that they will be exposed and found to be not good enough—a failure, rejected at their core. In this way, shame seeks secrecy. My own attempt was preceded by fear of exposure, judgment about my failed marriage, and unrealized career aspirations. I was, at the time, also cut off from all of my support systems. I was completely isolated from all but the family who originally shamed me.

Princeton psychologist, Silvan Tomkins, a pioneer in the development of what came to be known as affect theory, named nine basic emotions that we all experience. Each emotion is paired with its lesser and greater intensities, for example, anger–rage, fear–terror, shame–humiliation. We might think of toxic, or suicidal shame, as being located at the extreme end of the shame–humiliation pairing. Affect refers to the biological portion of an emotion; Tomkins's theory provided a link between the biology of the brain and the emotions we experience and express.[11]

Tomkins was not only interested in negative or painful emotions. Included in his list were two positive pairings: interest–excitement and enjoyment–joy, as well as one neutral affect, surprise–startle. He theorized that the shame–humiliation pair seemed to limit, or interfere with, the expression of other affects, especially positive pairings, such as excitement–joy.[12] I have observed this absence of excitement and joy in most of my clients suffering from what I call a "shame complex." I also experienced an absence of excitement and joy in my brother and, certainly, in myself.

Shame as Complex

Shame can become an identity that one takes on. This is why it constitutes a shame complex. We don't "have" shame as much as shame "has us." When a shame complex gets activated, an individual no longer feels separate from his or her shame—they ARE their shame. Many of their actions are, in turn, shame driven. This is because when shame is constellated, it takes over, or hijacks, the areas of the brain that control logical thinking. This was the case for me later in life when I went before the committee tasked with determining whether to certify me as a Jungian analyst. One of the members on the committee asked a question that I could not answer, and I was suddenly gripped by shame, and unable to reply coherently. I was blindsided by the strength and power of my own reaction. My brain was flooded, my executive functions shut down, and the shame rendered me profoundly helpless and humiliated. I wanted to run out of the room. Although I was eventually certified, I needed to do more work on my shame complex in my analysis.

Clinically, I have experienced this same crippling effect with clients, who avoid speaking up in social or professional situations, and even in therapy. They reveal little about themselves, and avoid intimacy. On the occasions when they are self-disclosing, or vulnerable, they often regret it afterward, and feel ashamed. Minor failures seem to prove their unworthiness. Mistakes, or slip ups, are expected to be followed by recrimination of some sort, and their "shameful" behavior is believed to reflect their inherent badness. Once individuals become aware of their complex, however, they can separate themselves from it and say, "That's just my shame complex; it's not me; it's not who I am." This refrain may be repeated hundreds of times over many years, but little by little, the shamed individual is able to chip away at the complex.

Shame versus Guilt

Shame is often confused with guilt, so it is important to note the distinction. David Lester, executive director of the Center for the Study of Suicide, points out that shame is a developmentally more primitive emotion than guilt. Unlike guilt, shame "encompasses the whole of ourselves and generates a desire to hide, disappear or die," says Lester.[13] Shame and guilt derive from different functions in the brain. Shame originates in the limbic system, while guilt is associated with the prefrontal cortex, and involves the logical and thinking parts of the brain.[14] The adrenaline produced by the prefrontal cortex helps us take action. When we feel guilty, we tend to judge our behavior as wrong or bad, and we are then able, based on our judgment, to apologize, or atone for our misdeeds. In this way, guilt is "a moral and adaptive emotion."[15] It makes us aware of our fallibility. According to some researchers, "Shame may represent the darker side of moral affect."[16] While the guilty person thinks, "I DID something bad," the shame-based person thinks "I *AM* bad." Repair, which involves thinking, and taking action, based on our thoughts, is difficult for someone with deep shame. Rather than reaching out, the shamed person tends to avoid contact, unless reaching out is to respond aggressively, or to respond defensively, as was the case with my brother.

Building on the work of Professor of Psychiatry, Michael Lewis, Kalafat and Kester explain that in cases of guilt, "we judge our behavior to be wrong, and we are able to apologize and perhaps atone for our misdeeds" whereas in cases of shame, "we feel that our whole self is no good, inadequate or unworthy."[17] The person who feels guilt can apologize and be forgiven. If forgiveness is offered, guilt is assuaged. Not so with shame. It is never assuaged, never forgiven. Recognizing shame only adds to the shame because even the feeling of shame is shameful.

Transmissibility of Shame

Some researchers, including Brené Brown at the University of Houston, use the term *lethal shame* to describe the kind of shame that can become suicidal, as opposed to momentary shame.[18] The two types differ in terms of both chronicity and intensity. Lethal shame leads to self-hatred and a desire to hide, run away, attack, avoid self-reflection, and even isolate—all risk factors for suicide. This kind of shame is transmissible and tends to run in families, often being handed down from one generation to the next, as was the case in my family. I have also seen this pattern in the clinical setting where suicidal clients identify at least one relative who killed him- or herself. In this way, shame begets shame, and suicide begets suicide. That is to say, not that everyone who feels shame is suicidal, but that shame in combination with other factors puts an already vulnerable individual over the top.

Because shame is handed down through the generations, some cultures are more shame-based than others. Asian cultures are particularly vulnerable. They not only fear shame in themselves, they also fear bringing shame upon their families. For Asians, suicide is an appropriate prophylactic. In the chapter on historical attitudes toward suicide, for example, I discuss the long tradition of suicide among Japanese Samurai warriors to avoid capture, and among Japanese women to avoid rape.

I have witnessed how mild shame initially becomes a motivation for success and living up to family and cultural values; however, over time, it can intensify to the point that it impedes the individuation process in some individuals. Unable to meet the high standards placed on them, these people may develop a deeper sense of shame than that intended by their families. Not uncommonly, clients of mine who suffer from this kind of culturally-based shame will express a desire to "end things," by which they mean to end their shame. One client told me on several occasions, "I just wish I wouldn't wake up." She had no specific, active plan to kill herself. Instead, she hoped some more powerful force would put an end to her misery. Once we were able to address the shame factor, she realized that she needed to end her *shame*, not her *life*. Until then, she was unaware of the degree to which she, and her entire family, suffered from shame, or of how to break the cycle.

Although many people claim that they would never kill themselves, citing their children as reason to stay alive, others believe that their children would be better off without them. Their shame interferes with their ability to understand why their death would be felt as a loss. I believe this to be the case with my brother, who felt that his own son would benefit from his death after a brief period of mourning. Perhaps, the family friend I mentioned in the first chapter also felt this way, as well as the parents of clients and friends of mine. One woman, who had lost her mother to suicide at thirteen, continued to carry her mother's shame into adulthood, and was able to stop the cycle only with her own child. Sometimes, having one parent who is not shame based can mediate the effect of shame by the other parent. If both parents carry a legacy of shame, as was true in my family, there is less likelihood that the children will come out unscathed. If, however, one or both parents become conscious of how they were steeped in shame, and have the ability to work on their shame, they are in a position to model recovery from shame for their children.

Shame and Difference

Individuals who are racially, neurologically, physically, emotionally, and gender divergent are frequent victims of shame—especially true of transgender individuals, and children and adolescents who experience severe bullying. Shame is often a factor in their suicides. The kind of shame they experience may be more akin to socially based shame, that is, shame emanating from society, rather than from parental shaming. The parents of such children, thus play an important role in diluting their children's shame, unless they, too, suffer from shame.

Too frequently, news stories tell us of a child who committed suicide after being bullied, or terrorized, on social media, or in school. Many such children felt too much shame even to confide in anyone, including their parents. One of the tragedies of shame is that it isolates a person so that they can't fight back, or seek help and support. Aloneness is one of the primary characteristics of shame. Often the parents will say of their child, "I had no idea what he/she was going through." Other times, parents will encourage their child to stand up for him- or herself, or to ignore what others say. Most children, especially those who don't fit into the norm, lack the ego strength not to internalize shame. Sometimes, the parents themselves feel shame about having a child who doesn't fit the norm, either consciously or unconsciously, and doesn't know how to respond. In the case of racial or ethnic bullying, the parents may have experienced the same shaming events, and either overreact, or underreact, to their own children's shame, having never developed effective ways of dealing with it themselves.

As a child, I was not physically or intellectually impaired, nor was I racially different, or gender divergent, but I was bullied and shamed for my emotional sensitivity at school, and then humiliated for it at home. These experiences laid the foundation for my shame complex. I often hear from suicidal clients how isolated and misunderstood that they felt as children because of some physical, or psychological infirmity, or perceived weakness. One woman told me that she was constantly planning ways to kill herself throughout her adolescence when, among other things, she was bullied by both kids, and the police, due to her ethnicity. She had no one to tell, least of all her immigrant parents, who worked several jobs just to survive.

With the proliferation of social media in this country, bullying and shaming has taken on greater significance, and become a source of an increasing number of suicides, even when the parents are caring and supportive. At the other end, we have seen police officers dishonored and shamed by the public to the point of killing themselves. We saw this when the four police officers, who tried to protect the United States Capitol on January 6, 2021, committed suicide. They may very well have felt shame and humiliation about their defeat.

As mentioned earlier, children and adolescents are at particular risk of being shamed. This is due, in part, to their lacking the coping skills, and judgment, of an adult, and of having little life experience to counter the attacks on them. While most of them survive adolescence, the shame they encountered when young may stay with them, and become yet another vulnerability and risk factor for suicide later—especially if compounded by later trauma or shaming events.

Shame and ADHD

One form of neurodivergence is attention deficit hyperactivity disorder (ADHD). Again, there is no direct link between ADHD and suicide, but there is a link between ADHD and shame. Unlike physical disabilities, ADHD and other "spectrum disorders" are invisible, and cannot be identified by appearance, but only by certain behaviors, which are viewed as unacceptable. For example, people with ADHD suffer from inattention, lack of focus and follow through, and emotional dysregulation, as do people with bipolar disorder. People with both diagnoses are also prone to impulsivity, which increases their chances of acting on a feeling. But instead of seeing these behaviors as a symptom of a neurological disorder, people tend to pathologize them, or think that they are just bad kids. Parents, teachers, friends, and partners accuse them of being lazy, selfish, and immature.

Suicide and Trauma

Naturally, many with ADHD internalize these negative labels, and feel shame.

Dr. Edward Hallowell, a pioneer in the field of treating ADHD, explains that shame raises hormone levels, and corrodes memory and executive functions. As a result, it is arguably the most painful of all symptoms associated with attention deficit disorder, he says.[19] Shame develops in the ADHD individual after years of feeling bad about behaviors he or she cannot control. Unable to manage their emotions, people with ADHD may lash out. Unable to focus, they may fail in school. Unable to remember what someone just said, they may incur the ire of parents and teachers. Over time, kids with ADHD lose friends, respect, and even trust—including trust in their own judgment. No wonder, children with ADHD feel flawed and unworthy. There seems no way for them to repair or redeem themselves.[20]

In working with clients who are shame based, and have ADHD, I help convert toxic shame into healthy guilt by teaching them to own what they did that made them feel ashamed, thus distinguishing doing from being. They may have done something "bad," but they are not, themselves, bad people. I also help them discern the true basis of their fears, since shame-based individuals either overreact, or underreact, to anticipated danger.

I have also observed a common relational pattern among sufferers of shame in general and those with ADHD. I call it the "shame-and-blame cycle." It is initiated when an individual is confronted about a behavior that someone else finds annoying, rude, or otherwise inappropriate. The offender has two choices: he can feel the shame and embarrassment and add it to the stockpile of other shaming incidents, or he or she can defend against the shame by blaming the other person and making it their fault, thus creating a wall of confusion, even gaslighting the person who shamed them. The latter may feel preferable from a self-esteem perspective, but the shame does not evaporate when we blame someone else. It simply dives down deeper into the unconscious. And relationally, it probably causes more problems than does accepting the blame, and feeling the shame. After all, no one wants to be counter blamed, or gaslighted—a sure way to end a relationship.[21]

My brother fit the diagnostic criteria for ADHD, although he was not formally diagnosed. I noticed this pattern of shame and blame in him early on. He tended to externalize his shame through the well-known defense mechanism of projection, in which a person projects onto others those parts that they reject in themselves. My brother projected so much shame and blame onto others that he began to believe his own projections, eventually developing fears that bordered on paranoia. He believed that most people could not be trusted, had ill intent, and wanted to harm him. He often talked about the people he hated. At the end of his life, he had few close relationships. Whenever a relationship failed, he blamed the other person. Inside, however, he perhaps blamed himself, which drove him further inward to avoid more rejection, and, in turn, led to more self-hatred through increased isolation.

The shame-and-blame dynamic is not specific to people with ADHD; many of us fall prey to this pattern. For reasons I've outlined previously, the shame and blame pattern appears to be more common in individuals diagnosed with ADHD, and bipolar disorder. It must be noted, however, that both conditions exist on a spectrum from mild to severe, and both can be helped by treatment—including with the shame.

Shame and Narcissism

Another condition related to shame is narcissism, especially covert, or hidden, narcissism, in which shame acts as a defense against early psychological wounding and insecurity. Unlike overt narcissism, or narcissistic personality disorder (NPD), covert, or "vulnerable," narcissism presents as seemingly more introverted, shy, and self-deprecating. In this condition, "Shame is more commonly felt than in overt narcissism," according to experts. "Whereas grandiose narcissism outwardly blasts others who threaten their ego, people with covert narcissism inwardly blast themselves and their own ego."[22]

The DSM does not distinguish among the various forms of narcissism. However, narcissistic tendencies in general are developed early in life when basic needs are not met. Psychologist Erik Eriksen (1902–1994), one of the first in the field to posit the existence of specific stages of psychosocial development, listed eight stages of development that occur over a lifetime: four of them take place in early childhood (before age twelve) and the other four develop over the remainder of one's life (twelve to sixty-five and older). Although it is possible to skip, or not complete, a given stage at the appropriate age, there are consequences for doing so, since each stage builds on the one before it.

Educator and researcher, Saul McLeod, explains that the first four stages that Eriksen identifies, in developmental order, are *trust versus mistrust, autonomy versus shame, initiative versus guilt,* and *industry versus inferiority*. The first stage: trust versus mistrust, tasks the child with developing a basic sense of trust, something that is accomplished by about eighteen months of age. Failure to accomplish this task may result in a general distrust of people, and of the world.[23]

The next challenge is to develop a sense of autonomy, which occurs between eighteen months and three years of age. McLeod states, "If encouraged and supported in their increasing efforts at independence, children will become more confident and secure in their ability to survive."[24]

If instead, McLeod goes on, the children are "criticized, overly controlled, or not given the opportunity to assert themselves . . . they begin to feel inadequate . . . and may become overly dependent upon others, lack self-esteem, and feel a sense of shame or doubt."[25]

Shame is thus the result of a failure to develop a healthy sense of autonomy.

During the next stage: initiative versus guilt, children learn how to interact with others, especially other kids at school. McLeod explains that "central to this stage is play, as it allows children to explore their interpersonal skills through initiating activities. . . . If given this opportunity, children develop a sense of initiative and feel secure in their ability to lead others and make decisions."[26]

Obstructions during this period may cause children to overdevelop their sense of guilt and discourage initiative. Of course, a certain amount of guilt is healthy and enables children to recognize when they have hurt or offended others, or broken some conventional or moral rule. In other words, healthy guilt enables children to develop a conscience. However, says McLeod, "Too much guilt can slow the child's interaction with others and may inhibit [his or her] creativity. . . . A healthy balance between initiative and guilt is important."[27]

According to Erikson, shame develops earlier than guilt. It is neurologically more primitive, as touched on previously in the section on the neurobiology of shame. Early shame can thus interfere with development of autonomy, and may compromise one's ability to develop a sense both of initiative, and of healthy guilt. Instead, the child gets stuck at a younger stage in development, unable to move from shame to guilt. This wounding, if pronounced, may cause the child to develop a personality disorder. In the case of narcissistic personality disorder, the healthy aspects of narcissism, the ability to move through the world with confidence rather than fear and shame, is compromised. And, as we have seen with ADHD, shame may be defended against, sometimes in unhealthy ways. Instead of taking responsibility for their actions, such children develop the coping mechanism of blaming others. Again, the goal is to help them replace unhealthy shame with healthy guilt.

In the case of a narcissistic disorder, and even covert narcissism, the prevailing feeling state that must be defended against is shame. The wounding to the ego develops so early in these disorders that a pattern of acting and reacting can become core to the personality, and is often hard to treat. Especially in cases of covert narcissism, the layers of protection against both guilt and shame are so thick that one risks fragmentation by making conscious that which would normally result in healthy guilt. At the same time, the sense of victimization can become so strong that one might well consider suicide, either for revenge, or for a need to prove themselves right. That is, because people with covert narcissism turn their feelings inward. They are more likely to identify as the victim, but they may also lash out in passive-aggressive ways, similar to people with borderline personality disorder.

In some ways, my brother met the criteria for covert narcissism, in that he had difficulty with self-reflection, a common feature in both shame and narcissism, and he tended to blame others while also fearing them, and being afraid to reveal his own true feelings out of a sense of shame. In addition, his suicide could be seen as an act of revenge against family members whom he felt did not respect him, or whom he envied. For him, dying may have been both a vindictive act, and a heroic one. One defense against covert shame is to seem heroic. Such people often give to others as a way of proving their virtue and worthiness, despite not having any real empathy for the recipient. For that reason, what they give is more often financial than emotional in nature.

Shame as an Impediment to Connection with the Self

The Self, as mentioned earlier, is the chief organizing principle of the psyche; it is the god within, a resource for good and ill that can guide us, support us, and help us manifest our wholeness, or completely overwhelm the personality. Katherine Best, in her article for the *Assisi Journal*, explains that shame disrupts the natural function of the Self, wherein the essence or heart of the Self is viewed as wanting.[28] As S. S. Tomkins has stated, "Shame is felt as an inner torment, a sickness of the soul."[29] Gershen Kaufman says The experience of shame is inseparable from man's search for himself,"[30] and Sandra Edelman describes shame as "a wound, searing pain, mortifying sense of degradation, total loneliness, terrifying, soul murder, horror, cursedness, torment, dread, and despair.[31] Philosopher, Friedrich Nietzsche, in answering the question What do you regard as most humane? said, "To spare someone from Shame. . . . To no longer feel ashamed in front of oneself." To Nietzsche, removal of shame is "the seal of liberation."[32]

Shame not only causes us to formulate negative and critical evaluations of ourselves, but also obscures positive evaluations. I remember a suicidal client who had an easier time looking at his negative qualities than accepting his positive aspects, which may have played a role in his decision to stop seeing me. He could not integrate the positive relationship he had with me, nor could he reconcile his bad feelings about himself with the good feelings about himself that were emerging in therapy. In his mind, sweetness belonged only to me, not to him. People with shame often have a hard time accepting compliments. They may feel incongruent with how the person feels about him- or herself, and are thus uncomfortable.

I, too, have struggled with compliments, especially about myself as a person. Such positive assessments have felt undeserving and misplaced. As a child, I felt valued only when I accomplished something. My core self was devalued to the extent that my natural feelings were discounted and pathologized. Many times, I was shamed when I simply tried to assert my authentic self or express legitimate feelings, both negative and positive. Whenever these true feelings were rebuked or mocked or I was scolded for having them, I internalized the message that there was something inherently wrong with me. For someone to see otherwise meant that I had put something over on them, that I was an imposter.

One memory in particular typifies the shame dynamic between my mother and me. At the time, I was in my early twenties. My maternal grandmother was in the hospital, dying. I'd come to visit her. My parents and other family members were also in attendance. My grandmother was crying out, "I don't want to die. I don't want to die." My mother, unable to bear her mother's pain or her own, left the room and fled down the hospital corridor. I followed her, wanting to comfort her. When I caught up with her, I reached my arms out to hug her. She pushed me away, ashamed of becoming so emotional, and rushed away from me, her arms flailing as if to say, "Stay away from me. Don't look at me, don't see my pain." I stood in the hall feeling ashamed of my desire to comfort her, and myself, physically with a hug. I felt small, and dirty, and embarrassed.

Not only did physical affection seem almost taboo in my family, but, more importantly, there was an absence of warmth. Many families may lack physical expressions of love, sometimes for cultural reasons, and yet, still maintain an atmosphere of warmth in the home, so that family members know they are loved and liked. I always wondered if I was.

Shame as Relationally Based

Allan Schore, and others, claim that chronic shame has its roots in early, repeated, right-brain experiences of affective dysregulation. Schore, a researcher and author of numerous books on interpersonal neurobiology at UCLA, notes the importance of small doses of shame in infant socialization, as well the need to mediate that shame through "interactive repair."[33]

Suicide and Trauma

Patricia DeYoung, whose work is based on Schore's theories, agrees that "interactive repair," namely, through a parent, is essential. DeYoung believes the source of shame is relational, and says emotional attunement is an essential ingredient in warding off shame. Without emotional attunement, one is set up for a lifetime of shame. This attunement, however, requires that the parent not be dysregulated him- or herself. Says DeYoung, "A dysregulating other is someone close to us whose emotional responses leave us feeling fragmented."[34] A parent who is overly anxious, or insecure, may be unable to attune to their child's feelings and needs.

An example of such an inadequacy is a young mother whose child was born while the father was away at war. Unable to manage her own fears and anxieties about her mothering capacities, she would yell, or slap, her infant daughter whenever she could not stop her from crying. She also stifled the child's natural curiosity. When the child became a woman, she grew to fear that her feelings were always a burden to other people, and felt much shame about her feeling states. While still quite curious, she refrained from asking too many questions, feeling that she would be seen as "too much."

Research shows that some people may be more vulnerable to chronic shame right from the start, depending on their temperament and predisposition. A mismatch between a child's needs, and the caregiver's ability to respond to them, is an important factor. I recognize this in my relationship with my own mother, whose logical and practical mind, combined with a kind of coldness and discomfort with physical affection, made her a bad fit for me—a sensitive and intuitive child in need of much physical and emotional soothing. I realize now that her insensitive parenting stemmed from her own shame and anxiety.

Over a lifetime, a sense of well-being for those suffering from chronic shame is highly dependent on the response of others. When outside response is good, they may feel important and valuable. When the response is negative, hurtful, or attacking, the shamed person slips back into feelings of worthlessness. Sadly, the negative state feels most congruent with who they are. Like me, many of my clients have suffered, not only from shaming comments and actions as children, but also from shaming behaviors in adolescence, and even adulthood. Shamed children can grow up to be shamed adults who, in turn, shame their children, who then may increase the shame their parent already feel, insulating the entire family in a web of shame.

Shame-based people work hard to appease others, but "their relationships are full of anger about disappointed expectations and dashed hopes," says DeYoung.[35] My brother was an example: he defended against his shame with anger at other people. DeYoung notes that shame is not located in the disowned parts of the Self, but in recurrent, powerful states of feeling horrible here and now. She states, "Such unbearable states fall into the background during periods of success, but when their self-esteem is attacked, shame becomes bitter, implacable anger, or intense anxiety."[36]

Mario Jacoby, however, believes the source of shame lies in the failure to heed one's conscience. He points out that the less self-confidence and self-esteem one has, the more likely one is to fall victim to intense shame to begin with.[37] Shame, to him, is internally driven, in contrast to the relational theories described above, in which primary importance is ascribed to the interaction between oneself and the other person. I believe both are sources of deep shame. Yet, I would interpret Jacoby's claim differently. A failure to heed one's conscience, or inner wisdom, may be felt as a sense of guilt, whereas the lack of confidence and self-esteem emanates from shame, which is both internally driven and externally reinforced.

Shame before God

Shame, as an experience, is described in our earliest myth, the fall from paradise, during which Adam and Eve are nakedly exposed before God. Their new consciousness after eating the forbidden fruit generates the need to stay hidden, in their awareness not only that they are different from each other (as male and female) but also that there is a third, namely God, who can see and judge them—and that makes exposure untenable. They are no longer alone, no longer *one*.

What this myth suggests, is that we can feel unworthy not only to other people, but to God. According to religious scholars, shame is a product of the consciousness of sin. Before God entered the picture, shame did not exist in Adam's and Eve's world. It is said in Genesis that the man and his wife were naked and felt no shame. What introduced the feeling of shame was God's judgment of them. Ever after, the story goes, we as humans have needed to hide ourselves from God, to cover our shortcomings, and to beg his forgiveness when we err.

Viewing childhood psychology in terms of the myth, as children, our *parents* are our gods. At least they seem so, for they carry the power to accept or reject us, to shame or support us. That is why early childhood experiences have such staying power. They can often seal forever our image of ourselves.

As a child, I received the message that I was unworthy in both my parents' eyes, and in the eyes of God. This message stemmed from my father's criticism of me that I wasn't Christian enough, and my mother's accusations that I was inherently unlovable because I was so selfish—the ultimate sin. From their disapproval, I deduced that not even God approved of me. It was a subtle message, but during my most shameful moments I felt that I did not deserve to live because of my inherent badness—at the same time, I didn't deserve to escape life, either. Instead, I had to suffer eternally. That was God's wish, the wish of a punishing God. My parents were his intermediary.

I have heard clients express these same feelings in our work together. I remember one client who often said she did not want to live whenever she fell into a shame spiral. She remembered being shamed by the nuns in Catholic school, who admonished her for watching a dove fly in the window instead of listening to the sermon. Experiences like this led her to feel inadequate before God, and further fueled existing feelings of worthlessness she had derived from her parents. Because her sister required more of their time and energy, she was left to fend for herself emotionally—something that was also true of my mother due to her early fragility, and of me as well after my brother was born.

The Christian God is not the only judging and punishing deity. A Muslim client of mine also experienced shame at the hands of a punishing god. Whenever bad things happened to her in life, they were considered her fault. Each incident was proof of how unworthy she was before God. Often, she felt guilty for having gotten an abortion when she was very young. During our work together, she became increasingly aware of an alternate, loving God in her psyche, who at times took a front seat to the punishing and shaming god. Whenever she fell into the clutches of the punishing god, I would remind her of the more loving, forgiving God, and note how both resided within her. She had a choice about which one to listen to.

In his book, *Legacy of Darkness and Light: Our Cultural Icons and Their God Complex*, Jungian analyst, Michael Gellert, points out that all three Abrahamic religions—Judaism, Christianity, and Islam—fall under the spell of the dark side of one God: Yahweh. As such, Gellert claims, "Many of our fathers have been instruments of God's dark side. That is because, psychologically speaking, they have lived under the roof of the same God . . . going all the way back to Abraham—the founding patriarch to whom the Abrahamic religions owe their origins."[38] Under the domination of such a God, feelings of shame and unworthiness in an individual may be pronounced.

In contrast to an outer god, Jungian psychology concerns itself with the *inner* god, which is what Jung termed the Self. The Self, as we have said, is that part within the psyche from which we derive a sense of who we are, and who we are destined to become. It is our source of meaning and purpose. Jung distinguished this "Self" from the more ego-based "self" with which we tend to identify. The Self, or inner god, is less intent on judging conventional morality, than on helping us develop our full potential, or wholeness. The Self, as the driving force toward individuation, is not as concerned with good and bad as it is with holding the tension of the opposites. It is amoral in that sense. Its moral authority is of a higher nature. Therefore, to live in relationship with the Self offers an opportunity to be relatively free of toxic shame, and of punishing gods.

It may be fair to say that when one is not connected to something larger than the ego, they may easily fall into depression or anxiety because the ego must always be fed, often from the outside. Shame does not feed the ego. It destroys it. That is why the shamed person needs the revitalizing resources of the Self.

In Jung's analysis of the Book of Job in the Old Testament, he examines Job's brutal encounter with Yahweh, and Job's struggle to assume his innocence and love of God despite God's seeming abuse of him.[39] Through Satan as intermediary, God, or Yahweh, takes from Job everything of value in order to prove to Satan that Job will not curse God, despite all his losses. It is a test of Job's loyalty. Psychologically, Job being tempted to curse God represents the temptation of the ego to inflate itself, and set itself above God/Yahweh, who, in this case, represents the Self.

At one point, Job confronts his suicidal despair, saying (Job 3:3–4):

> And the night *in which* it was said,
> 'A male child is conceived.'
> May that day be darkness;
> May God not seek it,
> Nor the light shine upon it.

His suicidal longings sound very much like those of someone faced with suicidal shame. Finally, he asks, (Job 3:23):

> *Why is light given* to a man whose way is hidden,
> And whom God has hedged in?

In this passage, we hear Job being forced to search for the meaning in his suffering, and it is that search which brings him to what we might call his first encounter with the Self. Jungian analyst, Edward Edinger, says, "In states of depression and despair, much of the libido which normally maintains conscious interest and vitality has sunk into the unconscious. This in turn activates the unconscious, causing an increase in dream and fantasy imagery."[40] Hence, we might assume, the appearance of God in the whirlwind. Here, Yahweh represents the dark side of the Self with which Job must come to terms, as do many people feeling suicidal, as he did.

Job learns to humanize God, and in turn, is redeemed by God. "To see the symbolic image behind the symptom immediately transforms the experience," says Edinger.[41] Thus, in that Job is led to the Self through his suicidal despair, he finds generative meaning in the despair after all.

According to Edinger, in such an encounter with the numinous, the archetypal reality underpinning conscious life is directly experienced by the individual. "Job's questions have been answered, not rationally but by living experience. It is nothing less than the conscious realization of the autonomous archetypal psyche; and this realization could come to birth only through an ordeal . . . a divine initiation process."[42] And again, "Because Job perseveres in questioning the meaning of the experience, his endurance is rewarded by a divine revelation. The ego, by holding fast to its integrity, is granted a realization of the Self."[43]

Hence, Satan, the catalyst for Job's suffering, ironically also sets in motion his redemption. As Edinger points out, Job's confrontation with the Self/Yahweh is an initiation of sorts in an archetypal pattern of death and rebirth, "analogous to all initiation rituals which attempt to bring about a transition from one state of consciousness to another."[44] It signifies the urge to individuation, which always involves breaking up the status quo, in order to bring about a new level of awareness and consciousness. In this way, Edinger says, Yahweh and Satan are working together.[45]

This new level of consciousness is represented in the story, perhaps, by Job's restoration to health, wealth, and well-being, not only for himself, but for all his descendants "to the fourth generation" (Job 42:16). Job's experience is indeed a powerful symbolic example of how the revitalizing resources of the Self can mitigate the negative effects on the psyche of shame.

Not until I entered analysis, did I became aware of the shame complex in me, or even that shame could form a complex. Nor did I have an experience of the Self. Through the process of a long analysis, I began to understand the relationship between shame and my own suicidal feelings, and I was able to utilize the positive resources of the Self in bringing new meaning to my experiences. For this reason, I believe Jungian psychology is uniquely equipped to deal with suicidal, or toxic, shame. That is not to say that shame magically disappears because of analysis, or any other intervention. It is a continuing struggle. The psyche continues to offer up new challenges, and to remind us that we are not fully healed. In addition, we may continue to struggle with other complexes, and shadow elements of our personality, throughout life. Hopefully, however, we will no longer be crippled by them.

8

SUICIDE AND DEPRESSION

Depression, suicide and creativity are related. . . . In the depressive state, there is a heightened sensitivity to the nuances of the human experience.
—Andrew Edmund Slaby

While depression is generally cited as the largest risk factor for suicide, it is one of the most treatable forms of mental illness. Yet, many people equate the two, believing that suicide is the result of depression. An informal definition of *depression* often means to feel sad, unmotivated, and lethargic. Depression, by itself, is not a mental illness. It must meet certain criteria as defined in the DSM to be considered a disorder. The criteria include persistent sadness, and loss of interest or pleasure, in daily activities that once brought joy. This psychological state must last a certain amount of time, and cause specific behavioral and physiological changes, including insomnia—something I suffered from during my own suicidal phase, which prompted me to procure the sleeping pills that eventually became the means for attempting to end my life.

Chronic insomnia, by itself, can give rise to suicidal feelings. In fact, a growing body of evidence has recently shown insomnia to be an independent risk factor for suicide among all age groups. According to one report that reviewed a cross section of studies, "A meta-analysis shows that the association between insomnia and suicide still holds, even after controlling for the presence or absence of depressive disorder and after controlling for the intensity of specific symptoms such as depressed mood and hopelessness."[1]

The first person to explore depression as mental illness was Sigmund Freud, who believed that the cause of depression lies in excessive self-blame, and guilt stemming from experiences in early life.[2] Freud's brand of psychology, psychoanalysis, was among the first to attempt a cure for this illness. Dr. Natalie Bernstein claims that "psychoanalysis understands depression as aggression that is too upsetting to manage or settle, so it is ultimately turned against the self (ego)."[3] She adds that when someone feels something is happening that they don't understand, a sense of inadequacy and self-blame may result.[4]

C. G. Jung, who followed on the heels of Freud, defined depression in terms of a loss of the libido, or life energy, that is not available to consciousness, but rather regresses into the unconscious, manifesting in memories, wishes and fantasies.[5]

Some might call the purpose of this a kind of regression into a symbolic womb is to make conscious certain unconscious contents for the purpose of rebirth, that is, to assimilate these contents into consciousness. Says Jung, "Depression should therefore be regarded as an unconscious compensation whose content must be made conscious if it is to be fully effective. This can only be done by consciously regressing along the

Suicide and Depression

depressive tendency and integrating the memories so activated into the unconscious mind—which was what the depression was aiming at in the first place."[6] In other words, depression has a psychological purpose, and understanding that purpose is part of the cure.

Both Freud and Jung predated the publication of the DSM, which defines depression more narrowly and specifically as including a combination of the following: depressed mood most of the day, nearly every day; diminished interest or pleasure in all or almost all activities; decrease in appetite or significant weight loss not due to diet; weight gain; insomnia or hypersomnia nearly every day, psychomotor agitation or retardation nearly every day; fatigue or loss of energy nearly every day; feelings of worthlessness or excessive or inappropriate guilt, as well as diminished ability to think, concentrate, or be decisive nearly every day; and/or recurrent thoughts of death or suicidality.[7]

We can see here the inclusion of previous ideas about depression, including Freud's suggestion that guilt is involved, and Jung's idea of a longing for death and rebirth, although the implication is not clearly stated in the DSM. What is added to the criteria is a minimum amount of time: two weeks, in which the symptomatology occurs almost every day. The DSM also distinguishes between a major depressive disorder, and a persistent depressive disorder, which the DSM refers to as *dysthymia*—a depressive disorder that lasts longer, but is less intense than a major depressive episode.[8] Dysthymia is more like a chronic, low-grade depression that rarely includes suicidality.

In addition, recent theorists, Jungian analyst James Hollis among them, have identified three basic classes of depression: *reactive*, *endogenous*, and *intrapsychic*. Reactive depression, also sometimes called "situational depression," is defined as a normal response to loss, or disappointment, and is often the most temporary. Endogenous depression is biochemical and/or genetically inherited; individuals with this form of illness seem to carry a certain "heaviness" in life that is palpable. The third form of depression, intrapsychic, refers to a kind of "pressing down of the life force," which is more akin to Jung's definition.[9]

My own depression fits into both the first and third categories. Although I was reacting to loss and disappointment, I was also experiencing a bottomless despair that had been pressing down on me, to some extent, since early childhood (reminiscent of dysthymia). However, I did not meet the requirements of a depressive disorder until the occurrence of the losses of both my career, and my relationships: first with my ex-husband, and then with Josh. It is well known that a child who has felt deeply betrayed, neglected, or abused by their parents, may later bond with someone, or many "someones," who will repeat the betrayal. In my case, it was my husband, and later my boyfriend, who reenacted the initial betrayal and abandonment by my father.

Treatment for moderate to severe depression may include anything from a few sessions of psychotherapy, to medication, and even hospitalization. Not all depression requires treatment, though. Life itself offers daily reasons for feeling depressed, as does loss, disappointment, failure, existential angst, and other so-called "negative" emotions. For the most part, these feeling states are temporary, but for some people, an intense form of the emotion may last days, weeks, or even years.

Depression is simply one way in which suffering is expressed among the animal kingdom, which includes humans.

Consider the number of elephants who grieve the death of a loved one, or whales who beach themselves when they've been separated from their pod. Although we can't ask whales about the depth of their feelings to determine their degree of depression, we can assume it by their actions. Of course, it is a different matter altogether for humans. Because of our ability to use language, it is possible to construct questionnaires to assess a person's level of depression based on specific criteria.

That's exactly what Aaron Beck did in 1961, when he designed a questionnaire based on certain "cognitive distortions" people might have that activate feelings of depression. The Beck Depression Inventory, a set of twenty-one questions, is a tool used for assessing a person's level of depression at any given time. Beck found that the seriousness of a person's intent to kill him- or herself correlated less with degree of depression, than with hopelessness about the future. In fact, one symptom listed in the DSM is hopelessness, and it is considered critical to a diagnosis of clinical depression. Mental-health professionals (and insurance companies), however, look at the overall score on the Beck Depression Inventory to make their determination, even though some symptoms may be more predictive of suicidality than others.

Mark Goldblatt at Harvard University agrees with Beck on the importance of hopelessness in assessing for suicidality. Goldblatt says, "For suicidal individuals, crushing hopelessness correlates more strongly than depression with suicidal intent."[10] Others, myself among them, believe that hopelessness as a general feeling is not as indicative of suicidality as is the *reason* for the hopelessness. In other words, what do the clients feel hopeless about? How long have they felt hopeless, and are there times when they don't feel hopeless? Knowing the answers to these questions helps determine the focus and direction of treatment. In my work with clients who express hopelessness, I pay particular attention to times, or situations in their life when they don't feel hopeless, and whether they are able to move in and out of hopeless states. It's when the feeling is all-encompassing that I become concerned.

Others prefer the term *despair* rather than *hopeless*. Despair adds additional elements to the sense of hopelessness. For example, James Hollis defines despair as being "without prospects, without alternatives . . . the worst of the dismal states for it seems to offer no way out."[11] Despair may result from a combination of aloneness, murderous hate, and self-contempt, or from the individual's inability to maintain, or envision, any human connections of significance.

Herbert Hendin, who wrote numerous books and articles on suicide, concluded that a combination of hopelessness, despair, rage, and guilt are among the emotions that have been shown to predominate in suicidal patients. Hendin was interested not only in the inner psychic factors, but also in the psychosocial contributors to suicide. He relied on dreams, as well as psychoanalytic interviews, to determine suicidality. Depression alone did not determine if a person was suicidal. He did not equate the two. He believed, in fact, as did both Freud and Jung before him, that most of the motivation for suicide stems from unconscious factors. Hendin also agreed with Freud on the importance of guilt in determining suicidality. Hopelessness, however, was a particularly salient factor to Hendin. But it could stem from outer as well as inner struggles.[12]

Suicide and Depression

A further element included in the definition of suicidal depression is that of desperation, which adds an element of urgency. In contrast to despair and hopelessness, both of which imply resignation, and a kind of acceptance of the situation, desperation portrays an acute sense that life is impossible without change. Desperation is also related to anxiety, which some say can fuel existing suicidal feelings. All these terms: *hopelessness, despair, desperation,* describe how I felt when I made my own suicide attempt. I simply could no longer bear the pain.

A word about resignation mentioned above: I have noted the sense of resignation in both myself, and others, at the time when we attempted suicide, which could account for the somewhat "freed-up" feeling that one experiences just before the actual attempt. Not only do people feel hopelessly defeated, but they seem to have accepted defeat—they are *resigned* to it. There is nothing more for them to do. The thought of killing themselves offers resolution and reduces anxiety. This ties in with the sense of desperation about the urgent need for some kind of radical change. I contend that the change needed is a psychospiritual shift; in the absence of such a shift, suicide seems to fit the bill. Suicide promises to assuage anxiety, depression, urgency, and hopelessness all at once.

Depression by itself tells us very little, and statistics claiming otherwise are misleading. Statistics also assume depression has a pathological connotation that can sometimes lead to an over-zealous rush to treatment, often with medication and/or hospitalization to quell the depressed feelings. One might ask, where is the real urgency—in the patient, the doctor, or both? The point is, that regardless of the term used: *depression, anxiety, hopelessness,* or *desperation*—the feelings of the suicidal person are real, and have a sense of immediate crisis about them, in contrast to those in a state of passive depression. People with suicidal depression do indeed need timely intervention, both human-to-human, and human-to-psyche.

Of course, not all theorists consider depression a pathological state. Some consider depression a necessary stage of growth and development, a signal that something requires our attention. Jungian psychologists, for example, use terms such as: the *defeat of the ego*, the *dark night of the soul*, or an *underworld experience*, not to mention an *initiatory experience*, to describe the necessary precursors to the individuation process—a process of becoming "whole." It is often the case that only after the ego has been defeated, does a person make a connection with what Jung calls the *Self*, the chief organizing principle of the psyche. Some would call this the *soul* or the *Higher Self*—that which is not always consciously available to us as a resource, yet is ever present. Sometimes the Self only emerges into consciousness during our darkest days.

Renowned analyst Esther Harding published a pamphlet-sized book in 1970 titled *The Value and Meaning of Depression*. In it, she claimed that the meaning meant to be found in the experience of depression, leads to the possibility of achieving wholeness. Like Jung, Harding said that the mechanism involved in depression is "a loss of libido, or energy." That energy disappears into the unconscious, and the "conscious life is left high and dry, sterile, arid, miserable and isolated."[13] Libido falls into the unconscious for a couple of reasons: either because its outward flow has been frustrated, constituting a regression, or because some unconscious content is demanding consciousness. The latter she calls a "creative depression," and says that the task is to recognize the nature of this unconscious content, and bring it into consciousness through a creative act. This is necessary because the unconscious content is a piece of one's wholeness that is buried in the unconscious. An example might be an unlived aspect of life needing to emerge at the expense of old, worn-out attitudes. It could be anything from a healthy amount of aggression, to awareness of a longing still stuck in the unconscious. However, the kind of depression I related to most was the depression that Harding considered more serious: "It [the depression] may be due to a block in one's whole life—the death of a loved one, the break-up of a marriage, serious illness, failure in business, or the collapse of all one's hopes and ambitions."[14]

It was not until years after my suicide attempt that I read Harding's work. In it, I discovered the meaning in my own depression. Huge sections of my wholeness had been held captive in the unconscious for some time before my suicide attempt. In fact, so little of myself was conscious that one could say I lacked a self, something therapists often talk about when referring to a very immature ego. People with little ego development, as I had at the time, cannot begin to see the bigger picture. They can't even see themselves clearly. I had no idea at that time what I might be capable of doing or feeling, in both positive and negative ways. I was simply a shell of the person I would later become.

Harding states that "when we fall into a severe depression, one that could truly be described as a night-sea journey or the valley of the shadow of death, perhaps the worst part of the experience is the loss of a sense of meaning. It seems that life has come to an end, and we might as well give up."[15] In my case, life had not even begun, but there were some dark forces within me that wanted me to give up.

Hollis acknowledges these dark forces in the psyche, but contends that "if we embrace despair and commit suicide, even then we have chosen. But we have chosen a path which admits no vital outcome." Instead, he says, "Staying alive, embracing despair and the awful pull of opposites, at least keeps open the possibility of resolution, of some forward movement."[16] He suggests that the task implicit in the encounter with despair is not to deny it but to "sustain the struggle . . . to suffer through toward whatever awaits beyond the tautologies of despair."[17] While I agree with him, I believe this is not a task one can take on in isolation—at the point of despair, an individual has no inner resources left. At least, he thinks he doesn't. Help in accessing the necessary resources must come from outside of the suicidal person, at least initially.

Psychologist Katherine Best, who has written at length about suicide, says, "The 'dark night of the soul' is the death experience of an old pattern or lifestyle, as the new way of living is gasping to be born, the soul crawling towards transformation like a butterfly emerging from a cocoon."[18] Her approach to suicidal clients is first to help them look for a way to die symbolically, rather than physically. To a client who is contemplating suicide, she asks, "What really needs to die? A relationship? A false belief? A social mask or role? Physical power? Your shame?"[19]

After my own suicide attempt, it became apparent that I held some archaic ideas about relationship, as well as beliefs about my personal worth, and my possibilities for happiness. These old beliefs had to die, at least symbolically, which means psychologically. Ironically, my mother commented on the short life of a butterfly just days before her death at seventy-two. It struck me because it seemed so out of character for her, as if her insight was coming from some place in her other than her practical, logical self—some spiritual realm, perhaps. After that, the butterfly became an emblem of transformation for me, reinforced by a dream I had soon after my mother's death, in which she was drawing a beautiful butterfly with colors I had not imagined. Perhaps she was crawling toward transformation after death in the same way that I was crawling toward it in life.

Best suggests that "turning away from suicide calls for an active transformational experience of surrendering or sacrificing something either symbolically or real. Whatever has become a barrier or obstacle for our body and soul to engage in a sacred relationship of respect and care may have to be released."[20] Being with the client through this process in a respectful, and nonjudgmental, way is essential to healing, says Best. That means going the distance. Only then, can transformation occur naturally, and with grace and support.[21]

David Rosen, a psychiatrist and Jungian analyst, talks about the necessity of what he calls "ego-cide"—an antidote to suicide. Rosen says that what needs to die in suicidal clients is their distorted relationship to their ego, or conscious sense of identity. Instead of killing themselves, they need to make a shift from an ego identity to a larger sense of Self. "This process feels like dying, so it sets in motion a kind of mourning process. Once the mourning for the lost dominant ego-identity is complete, the person experiences 'New Life,' an existence that is more promising than the one left behind," according to Rosen.[22] This rebirth he calls *transformation*. The ability to transform shame into a sense of purpose is critical.

Take, for example, the person who suffers from deep shame, as I did. What is needed to transform that shame into a sense of purpose involves developing a relationship with the Self, and working to shatter the negative mirror image provided by the outer world—or by what Jungians call a complex. In place of negative images and beliefs, one must construct more positive valuations, based on the knowing of the Self.

Interviewing survivors who jumped off the Golden Gate bridge, Rosen found that their motivation to kill themselves was steeped in profound feelings of aloneness, alienation, depression, rejection, worthlessness, and hopelessness—feelings we discuss throughout this book. Yet, the moment their feet left the bridge, the jumpers regretted their choice, feeling they had made a mistake. None of the people he interviewed (six of the eight who had survived) ever made another attempt at that spot, or anywhere else.[23] One can speculate that in that lethal moment, the Higher Self was screaming, "No! Don't kill me!" According to Rosen, they "all admitted to feelings of spiritual transcendence after they had leaped."[24]

What Rosen discovered was that, after their death leap, each of the survivors managed to undergo a "symbolic suicide."[25] That is, they were able to let those parts of themselves that were causing them pain *die*, and then to grieve their loss. The ten individuals who set out to commit suicide "had somehow cleared the way for psychic regeneration (and) had symbolically killed their previous negative ego identities," says Rosen. "Through the act of surviving their depressive and suicidal states, they had transformed themselves."[26]

Jungian Analyst, Marion Woodman, asserts that without transforming, one is bound to a kind of psychic suicide. Using the butterfly image as an example, she explains what happens when a person gets stuck in the chrysalis, unable to make the shift necessary for psychic regeneration and transformation:

> Birth is the death of life we have known; death is the birth of the life we have yet to live . . . people stuck in a perpetual chrysalis are in trouble. Stuck in a state of stasis, they clutch their childhood toys, divorce themselves from the reality of their present circumstances and sit hoping for some magic that will release them from their pain into a world that is just and good, a make-believe world of childhood innocence. Fearful of getting out of relationships that are stultifying their growth, fearful of confronting parents, partners or children who are maintaining infantile attitudes, they sink into chronic illness and or psychic death. Life becomes a network of illusions and lies. Rather than take responsibility for what is happening, rather than accept the challenge of growth, they cling to the rigid framework that they have constructed or has been assigned to them from birth. They attempt to stay fixed. Such an attitude is against life, for change is a law of life.[27]

This last sentence recalls what I said in chapter 6 about the law of life versus "God's law." The law of life here is that everything must change or die.

Clarissa Pinkola Estés talks about depression in poetic terms, referring to it as "instinct injured." In *Women Who Run with the Wolves*, Estés writes about what happens to women who have lost their instincts, becoming overly domesticated, and no longer connected to their wildish nature and to their soul. Without openly criticizing such women, she points out that "lack of fleeing when it is absolutely warranted causes depression. . . . Too much domestication breeds out strong basic impulses to play, relate, cope, rove, commune, and so forth."[28] Her rich stories of the Wild Woman archetype paint a clear picture of what leads to depression, and what leads out of it.

In her story of "Bluebeard," it is the inner predator that is the culprit. "In the instinct injured woman, the predator is upon her before she registers its presence," says Estés. The cure, for both the naive, and instinct-injured woman, is to "practice listening to your intuition, your inner voice; ask questions, be curious; see what you see; hear what you hear; and then act upon what you know to be true."[29]

After discovering my own naive, instinct-injured woman within, I was better able to honor and listen to my inner voice and to trust my intuition that, as a child, was often maligned. I became increasingly aware of what felt right, and what felt wrong—without needing to constantly defend my "feeling."

In Estés' discussion of "The Ugly Duckling," I resonated with what she says about the role of the mother in the internalization of feelings such as: shame, doubt, and aloneness, which freezes creativity. The way out is to find one's own flock, a metaphor for finding the inner and outer voices that recognize, and value, your own unique self. Her stories offer women (and some men) a way of reframing their suffering in a meaningful way that does not pathologize it. Like so many analysts and therapists who approach suicide by humanizing it, Estés offers a symbolic and human way of approaching and understanding suffering.

It must be noted that there are biological and neurological abnormalities that cause depression, and are not amenable to psychological or psychotherapeutic approaches, at least not as the sole treatment. I discussed some of these factors in appendix C. In addition to those mentioned, a lack of mature brain development may play a part in suicides among young people, as the brain is not fully developed until about age twenty-six. Consequently, younger people may be more impulsive and more prone to poor judgment. Certainly, they lack awareness of the bigger picture. Trauma may also play a role in suicides of young people. Emotional trauma may result from poor parenting, bullying, and undeveloped coping skills to deal with even minor challenges. Nevertheless, some people, even with physiologically based impairments, can benefit greatly from traditional psychological approaches, sometimes in conjunction with medication, and sometimes without it.

9

SUICIDE AND TRAUMA

Trauma by nature drives us to the edge of comprehension, cutting us off from language based on common experience or an imaginable past.

—Bessel Van der Kolk

While trauma itself is not a mental illness, the effects of it can be. In 1980, the American Psychiatric Association added post-traumatic stress disorder (PTSD) to its existing list of mental disorders. Previously, child abuse, war, and other traumatic events, were thought to cause anxiety and depression, even psychosis; traumatized individuals were treated for those diagnoses, depending on which one was most prevalent, or severe. If, for example, a traumatized child or adult showed symptoms of anxiety, they were treated for anxiety; if they showed symptoms of depression, they were treated for depression. By adding post-traumatic stress disorder to the DSM, the source of their anxiety and depression could both be addressed under one diagnosis: PTSD.

World War II first brought PTSD to the attention of the psychiatric community. Psychiatrists noted that war itself caused a predictable array of symptoms common to returning soldiers, and assigned it a name. Since then, the diagnosis of PTSD has been refined and clarified to include many other types of traumas unrelated to war. The American Psychiatric Association estimates that about 3.5 percent of adults are affected by PTSD each year, and that one in eleven people will be diagnosed with it in their lifetime.[1] Not all people who suffer from trauma, though, meet the criteria for PTSD. Acute Stress Disorder (ASD) is defined by similar symptoms, although may begin three days to a month following the traumatic event. About half the people with ASD are later diagnosed with PTSD. Of the individuals who experience interpersonal violence, 19 to 50 percent are diagnosed with ASD. Many others who experience trauma may not fit a particular diagnosis, but they suffer nevertheless—emotionally, physically, and spiritually.

The word *trauma* in modern society is often used loosely as a descriptor, as in "I was traumatized," or "It was traumatizing." We may use it as a noun: "The trauma he suffered was horrific," or "She has been suffering from trauma since her accident." Such wordage recognizes that the symptomatic response: anxiety, depression, hypervigilance, substance abuse, etc., is a direct result of a particular kind of event. A traumatizing event, however, does not affect everyone the same way. Not everybody who goes to war, for example, returns with PTSD, even though they may speak of the experience as traumatizing.

Some experts claim that there are no objective criteria that can adequately evaluate events as traumatizing. It is simply a question of one's reaction to the event, not the event itself. We do know that traumatizing circumstances typically involve loss of control, betrayal, abuse of power, helplessness, pain, confusion, and/or loss—as in the sudden loss of a loved one.

"The event need not rise to the level of war, natural disaster, nor personal assault to affect a person profoundly and alter their experiences," says one authority. "Traumatic situations that cause post-trauma symptoms vary quite dramatically from person to person. Indeed, trauma is very subjective, and it is important to bear in mind that it is defined more by its response than its trigger."[2] Nevertheless, the addition of PTSD to the lexicon has resulted in our taking certain events, or triggers, seriously in and of themselves.

Antonieta Contreras, a licensed social worker specializing in trauma in New York, lists several different kinds of traumas, each affecting the autonomic nervous system (ANS) in different damaging ways. Here is her list:

Attachment Trauma, which occurs when there is a mis-attunement, or no attunement at all, between mother and child, which Contreras says results in an inability to regulate and balance the branches of the ANS.

Developmental Trauma, which is similar in that it stems from a lack of comforting, and of meeting a child's basic needs, resulting in nervous-system confusion, overactivation of the parasympathetic nervous system (PNS), and the manifestation of psychiatric symptoms such as dissociation, depression, and learning disabilities.

Complex Trauma, defined as caused by stressful, recurrent, and prolonged events, which causes one branch of the ANS to override the other, resulting in hyper- or hypo-arousal.
Racial Trauma, the result of fearing the impact of one's participation in society due to skin color, similar in effect to complex trauma but possibly more acute in its expression.
Historical or *Intergenerational trauma*, which occurs when the parent's level of anxiety is so high that it interferes with the child's developmental progress and self-image.[3]
Both racial and intergenerational trauma may carry a shame component that further affects self-esteem, and causes confusion about where one belongs—that is, about one's place in the world.

Other researchers define trauma as acute, chronic, or complex.[4] Some distinguish between physical and emotional trauma.[5] The effects of these kinds of traumas may differ, as may the effects of spiritual trauma wherein a child or adult may be traumatized by their spiritual training. Some experts categorize trauma by its source, such as a severe illness, violent or sexual assault, traumatic loss, mugging or robbery, car or plane accident, witnessing a terrible attack or natural disaster, being victim of a terrorist attack, hospitalization (including psychiatric), military combat, childbirth, life-threatening illness or diagnosis, and post-suicide attempt.[6] Still others categorize trauma by how a person responds to it, including fight, flight, freeze, or fawn.[7]

In my research, I found a wide range of definitions for the word *trauma*. For example, one source said that psychological trauma is a response to an event that a person finds highly stressful or distressing.[8] We might include in this definition taking the Bar, or some other high-stakes exam, or even driving on the freeway during rush hour, which most of us would not think of as particularly traumatizing. Another source defines trauma as a psychological reaction to a harmful or life-threatening occurrence that is outside the normal experience and beyond one's control.[9] That source does not define "normal" experience, but adds the dimension of helplessness.

Another way to define trauma is as a psychological or emotional response to an event or experience that is "deeply disturbing." The response to trauma can range in severity. A person can be a little traumatized, or highly traumatized. Several sources say that the intensity of the condition—a disordered psychic or behavioral state—determines whether something is traumatic.

A more specific definition of trauma is the response to a deeply distressing or disturbing event that overwhelms an individual's ability to cope, causing feelings of helplessness, diminishment of a sense of self, and an inability to feel a full range of emotions.[10] This definition focuses on what happens to the person, instead of focusing on the nature of the traumatizing event. It addresses the person's inner experience. I find this definition the most useful for our purpose in talking about trauma and suicide.

PTSD and the DSM

In the 1950s, psychiatrists created the Diagnostic and Statistical Manual of Mental Disorders (DSM), which has been periodically updated as we learn more about the nature of a given condition. It offers a uniform way of diagnosing patients who suffer from mental illness. The DSM defines post-traumatic stress disorder as the result of exposure to actual or threatened death, serious injury, or sexual violence in the following ways: direct experience, witnessing it as it happens to others, learning that it has happened to a close family member or friend, or experiencing repeated or extreme exposure to aversive details of a traumatic event.[11]

Symptoms include the presence of intrusive thoughts or memories, recurrent dreams, dissociative reactions, prolonged distress after exposure to internal or external events resembling or symbolizing the original event, and demonstration of a marked reaction to those events. Other symptoms include avoidance behaviors and alterations in cognition, mood, and memory. While the DSM seems to omit nonviolent emotional, or psychological, distressing events in its definition, research shows that one need not be exposed to violence to experience PTSD.

While not everyone who has experienced a traumatic event meets the criteria for PTSD, we know that trauma leaves a trace, not only on the psyche, but also on the brain. With the development of neurobiology, and other brain-based sciences, we know that trauma is not just an experience; nor is it just a feeling response to an event, or a cluster of behaviors—it has neurological manifestations. That is, there are actual physical changes in the brain that occur because of trauma.

Trauma and the Brain

In study after study, post-traumatic stress, as well as emotional trauma, tend to affect three areas of the brain: the amygdala, the hippocampus, and the prefrontal cortex.[12] All three areas of

Suicide and Trauma

the brain play a role in regulating emotions, and responding to fear. The amygdala, as we saw in the chapter on shame, aids in perceiving and controlling emotions. It gathers information in the environment that might present a threat of some kind. Upon sensing a threat, a feeling of fear is produced. The amygdala becomes hyperactive. Thereafter, when either a literal, or symbolic, similar event happens, the amygdala will again become hyperactive, leading to a state of chronic stress, heightened fear, increased irritation, and difficulty calming down, sleeping, or remembering.

The ventromedial prefrontal cortex is responsible for executive functioning, that is, higher level thinking and reasoning. When the prefrontal cortex senses fear, it will react rationally, at least initially and under normal circumstances. During extreme trauma, however, the fear response may override a person's otherwise rational mind, and compromise higher-level thinking skills.

The little place in the brain called the hippocampus may in turn affect a person's ability to recall memories of the trauma. Studies reveal that the volume of the hippocampus is smaller in trauma survivors, which may explain why a victim may not be able to differentiate past trauma from a current threat, and thus activate a fight-or-flight response to a current threat as if it were the original. [13]

Many years ago, I dated a Vietnam veteran. Every Fourth of July, the city displayed fireworks over the nearby pier. On one such occasion, as we walked along the beach toward the pier, my boyfriend suddenly dove into the sand, covering his head. For a few moments, he was back in Vietnam. Afterward, he apologized, feeling embarrassed, and disoriented. At the time, the term PTSD was just becoming more known, especially among war veterans. He had been diagnosed with PTSD, and was on disability.

Damage of any kind to the brain can affect one's ability to process and store information, which is essential to memory. The amount of memory loss depends on the degree of brain damage. In turn, the damage to the brain depends on the frequency, and intensity, of the trauma. The term *dissociative amnesia* refers to the inability to remember important information about one's life. The amnesia can be mild, or severe. It may also be temporary, or long lasting. A person who is physically and/or sexually assaulted may remember few details of the encounter, even years later, whereas someone who experienced a car accident may initially forget important details, but have their memory return with time. With treatment, even severe trauma may be treatable to the extent that victims can retrieve more and more of their memory. This has proven true with many Vietnam vets.

In chapter 11, I will discuss a client of mine who fell several stories from a building when she was a child, and suffered multiple wounds. She was unable to retrieve any memory of the accident, but was besieged much of her life by dreams of falling, including a dream of falling through the earth.

Trauma not only affects people emotionally and psychologically, but has a profound impact on their ability to relate to others. The traits of difficulty regulating emotions, and the inability to trust, are made worse by trauma, thus rendering it a challenge for such individuals to sustain long-term relationships. Veterans of various wars, who were unable to manage their PTSD, have exemplified this condition, resulting in an untold number of divorces. In such cases, not only does the soldier suffer, but often their family also suffers a kind of secondary trauma as they witness the irritability, fear, rage, and depression of their loved one. Thus, the whole family may be indirectly traumatized. This was certainly the case for me while married to someone with undiagnosed PTSD following his tour of duty in Vietnam.

Similarly, adults who experience severe trauma at the hands of parents, or other caretakers, find it difficult to attach to another person. Trauma victims may be avoidant, or abusive, themselves—something that we are more aware of today. In my husband's case, he was traumatized by child abuse long before he went to war.

Childhood Trauma

Trauma varies in terms of type, severity, and duration. Not surprisingly, those who have encountered multiple traumas, or the same trauma repeatedly over a period of years, are more prone to trauma's adverse effects than are those who experience a single episode, or mild trauma. However, this is not always the case as a severe trauma at a certain age, and under certain circumstances, may result in debilitating effects equal to multiple traumas.

Living with untreated trauma can create such inner and outer chaos and turmoil that the traumatized individual is driven to suicide. In studies on the effects of childhood abuse, researchers found a strong link between physical, or sexual, abuse and later suicide. One study found that adults with history of abuse are twenty-five times more likely to commit suicide than those without an abuse history. In that study, 21 to 34 percent of participants, who reported a history of abuse or neglect, made a suicide attempt, compared with 4 to 9 percent without such a history.[14] The link is strongest among those who have experienced sexual abuse, including 9 to 20 percent of suicide attempts by adults, and this statistic is independent of other known risk factors, including psychopathology.[15] This suggests that the trauma itself puts one at risk of suicide. The authors found that males, who have been sexually abused as children, are at an even higher risk of suicide than females. However, when sexual abuse occurs before age sixteen, women are three to four times more likely to attempt suicide than women abused after age sixteen.[16]

A study on the relationship between childhood trauma and the risk of suicide among incarcerated women also showed a strong link between childhood experience and suicidal feelings. Among the female prisoners in the study, 58 percent reported emotional abuse, 54 percent reported physical abuse, 51 percent reported sexual abuse, 53 percent reported emotional neglect, and 41 percent reported physical neglect.[17] The authors found that factors independently associated with past suicide attempts in this population included higher childhood-trauma scores. They concluded that "childhood trauma is an independent risk factor for attempted suicide among women in prison that persists into adulthood and cannot be fully attributed to psychological distress, illicit drug use, or incarceration duration."[18] Again, the experience of trauma puts individuals at a high risk for attempting, or completing, a suicide.

Pervasiveness of Trauma

Trauma is much more common than one might think. Some researchers estimate that 60 to 75percent of people in North America experience a traumatic event at some point in their lives.[19] The UK charity, Mind, lists the following as potential causes of trauma:
- bullying
- harassment
- physical, psychological, or sexual abuse
- sexual assault
- traffic collisions
- childbirth
- life-threatening illnesses
- sudden loss of a loved one
- being attacked
- being kidnapped
- acts of terrorism
- natural disasters
- war[20]

A survey conducted by the World Health Organization reported that at least one third of the more than 125,000 individuals surveyed in twenty-six countries had experienced trauma. The number rose to 70 percent when the group was limited to people experiencing core disorders as defined by the DSM-IV.[21] That number reflects only reported instances; the actual number is probably much higher. Note that psychological abuse is included on the list created by Mind. Many people are traumatized by verbal abuse, ridicule, and gaslighting, which is also a form of trauma. In fact, adults, who experienced physical abuse as children, claim that the emotional abuse that accompanied the trauma, was worse than the physical pain.

Other Types of Trauma

Beginning in childhood, trauma can occur at any point in life, and each trauma that a person experiences, compounds any past traumas. A person, who experiences abuse as a child, may then as an adult, confront a natural disaster, war, or other horrible trauma. If not treated, one's entire life may eventually feel traumatic. My ex-husband is one of the many veterans who suffer from PTSD, who have also endured childhood trauma. As a child, he experienced physical and emotional abuse, neglect, abandonment, and rape before he was shipped off to Vietnam, where he had to engage in battle. Although the PTSD he suffered was attributed to war, the source of his trauma was multiple and complex, and preceded the trauma of combat.

Research also shows that the more trauma a person experiences, the more likely they are to develop physical and psychological problems that may lead to suicide. As we have seen, trauma, like shame, affects the brain. Trauma also puts people at a higher risk of developing physical illnesses such as: chronic liver, lung, and heart disease, cancer, viral hepatitis, autoimmune disease, sexually transmitted infections, and alcoholism, to name a few. Trauma causes the body to produce excessive amounts of adrenaline and cortisol, which can reduce immune responses. A weakened immune system, in turn, can lead to increased infections. Trauma victims may also develop self-soothing habits that compromise their health, such as eating unhealthy food, drinking alcohol, taking drugs, or smoking.

The DSM lists the following physical effects associated with trauma: sweating, shaking, headaches, dizziness, stomach problems, general aches and pains, chest pain, and sleep problems. Several studies show a relationship among PTSD, sleep disturbance, and suicidality. Some even suggest that sleep disturbance may predict suicide in veterans. Researchers found that sleep disturbance can be a suicide warning sign when they studied a sample of veterans, who died by suicide shortly after seeing a doctor about their sleep problems. The research indicated that sleep disturbance might provide an important intervention target for at-risk veterans.[22]

Additional Research on Suicide and Trauma

We have seen how childhood trauma puts people at risk of suicide, as does war and other catastrophic events. The question is whether those formally diagnosed with PTSD differ in any way from other traumatized individuals. Researchers at Auburn University discovered that the most telling symptoms of suicidal ideation are detachment and estrangement from others. These symptoms differ from avoidance, which is a coping strategy invoked to escape trauma stimuli. The researchers call detachment and estrangement "numbing" symptoms that arise "outside an individual's deliberate control" and are "a consequence of chronic hyperarousal." Numbing, they say, is associated with greater pathology and interpersonal difficulty, distress, and the deterioration of social networks. They suggest that "numbing, rather than avoidance, may be linked to the development of suicidal ideation.[23] This study, and others like it, suggest that there may be more to learn about the relationship of PTSD, trauma in general, and suicidality.

Kendra Thorne, a certified rehabilitation counselor, and doctoral candidate in educational psychology and learning systems at Florida State University, wrote an article on traumatic stress and suicide examining the relationship between post-traumatic stress symptoms and suicide in rural areas. Among her research findings, Thorne discovered that suicide rates in rural areas are nearly double those in urban areas. She claims that limited access to health care is an important factor. Individuals in rural areas are also more reluctant to seek help after experiencing trauma. In addition, they tend to have higher rates of disability. Finally, even though the two groups have similar levels of suicidal ideation, people in rural areas are more likely than those in urban areas to have firearms, which are used as a highly effective means to commit suicide. Commenting on her findings, Thorne says, "People with trauma histories develop these fear networks, and so these networks include stimuli that's associated with the trauma, and physiological and emotional reaction to the trauma, and then interpretations and meaning." She adds that this "fear network" will remain intact "unless some new learning occurs."[24] This study underscores the importance of education, and access to mental-health opportunities, as well as the effect of disability as a risk factor for suicide. It also raises concern about the increasing access to firearms, the most lethal means of suicide.

On the other hand, people in rural areas, especially agricultural communities, depend on each other in ways people in cities, and even small towns, do not. Rural communities tend to have a closer sense of connection than do urban dwellers, which may aid in recovering from trauma. Despite the relative physical isolation, there is an "everyone knows everyone mentality."[25] Since isolation is a risk factor for suicide, the feeling of "being known" to others may lessen suicidal feelings for some people.

The sense of shared interests and needs, and the tendency to socialize with others, who are close in proximity, helps them feel at home. Often, they, and those nearby, have known one another and their families for generations. This kind of "knowing" presupposes acceptance and support.

At the same time, those who have suffered from trauma may not want anyone to know "their business," and this can have the reverse effect of their desire to isolate even more. Perceived judgment of others can contribute to a sense of aloneness, shame, low self-esteem, and other negative emotions, which can lead to suicide. The latter describes the effect that living in a small town held for me. As my own experience shows, having a small, close-knit community is not always a mitigating factor.

Mitigating the Effects of Trauma

Since we know what causes trauma, and how it effects individuals physically, emotionally, and relationally, how do we mitigate its negative effects so that the traumatized person doesn't resort to suicide? Most experts agree that the first step is to recognize the tendency toward trauma. As mentioned earlier, the effects of trauma may first appear as anxiety, depression, and PTSD. In fact, when someone seeks treatment, they may initially be diagnosed with a standard disorder. However, therapists quickly learn that to treat *one* of the symptoms (anxiety, depression, alcoholism—even suicidal ideation) is not enough. A therapist must treat the entire cluster of symptoms. And beyond that—tend to the soul.

Over the years, different techniques have emerged to treat trauma. Immersive therapy was an early treatment option, in which individuals are exposed to triggers that mimic the original trauma. Immersive therapy was used with veterans of war. For some, immersive therapy exacerbated the problem; for others, it has brought lasting peace. Psychotherapist, Edward Tick, and author of *War and the Soul: Healing Our Nation's Veterans from Post-traumatic Stress Disorder*, continues to lead American war veterans on reconciliation pilgrimages to Viet Nam. There, much to the Americans' disbelief, they are often warmly praised for their bravery by former Vietnamese Communists, or The Viet Cong. Many American veterans have since helped build medical clinics and schools in the country of their one-time enemy, which is as healing for their souls, and beneficial for the Vietnamese people.[26]

In recent years, brain-oriented restructuring therapies have come into vogue: Eye-movement desensitization and reprocessing (EMDR), and magnetic-resonance therapy, are now used in addition to talk therapy, and traditional approaches to treat PTSD such as: cognitive processing, exposure therapy, and medication.

While these individual techniques result in improvement for many individuals, the technique explored is not as essential as the patient's relationship with the health-care professional, especially when it comes to suicidality resulting from trauma. Trauma erodes the ability to trust, attach, communicate, and feel safe. To develop a relationship with a healthcare professional, especially over time, helps to rebuild trust, increase the ability to attach and communicate, and to feel safe. In essence, trauma work at its best is relationship work, and soul work.

10

TRANSFORMATION
An Unconscious Human Longing

Every transformation demands as its precondition "the ending of the world"—the collapse of an old philosophy of life.

—C. G. Jung

Jungian analysts are fond of talking about transformation, individuation, and the integration of opposites. The integration of opposites is critical to individuation. Without it, a personality may be one sided. Take, for example, someone who holds a conscious attitude about themselves as being kind and generous. They may very well possess kind and generous qualities, but they may also be unconscious of opposing traits, including tendencies to be unkind, stingy, or withholding. The person would prefer to identify with the conscious qualities, rejecting the nasty, unconscious elements. But those elements will nevertheless continue to exist in the *shadow*—which, as discussed earlier, Jungian psychology understands as that part of the unconscious that contains all the tendencies (positive as well as negative) that we don't want to acknowledge in ourselves. To put it simply, the shadow is comprised of those qualities "a person has no wish to be."[1] In the process of transformation, though, all such tendencies are brought to consciousness and integrated into the personality, rather than split off—this integration leads to wholeness.

Too often, we are plagued by our shadow. We tend to disown the unwelcomed personality characteristics that would embarrass us, and instead of integrating the characteristics, and accepting them as part of who we are, we project them onto other people.

In my relationship with Josh, he projected his own "sensitive," and overly emotional shadow side, onto me. Like Josh, when we project our shadow onto other people, we are not even conscious of doing so—it is automatic. Shadow parts are simply too distasteful. On the other hand, when we are able to integrate them into consciousness, we become more fully human, and empathic. We can accept the less-than-admirable qualities in others when we can accept them in ourselves.

Jung described the process of individuation in metaphoric language, using alchemical terms. He saw a parallel between what the early alchemists were attempting to do with physical reality (transform lead into gold) and what humans were attempting to do psychologically (transform the personality). Jung adopted the term: *prima materia* (first matter) from the alchemists, who borrowed it from Aristotle to describe pure potentiality, meaning that which exists before taking form. Jung applied the term to describe the transformation of fixed aspects of the personality.

"First matter is the name of that entirely indeterminate power of change," according to Aristotle.[2] Before anything can be transformed, it must first be reduced to its original, undifferentiated state, or *prima materia*. Returning these aspects to that undifferentiated state is part of the process of individuation, according to Edward Edinger.[3] He talks about the prima materia in *Anatomy of the Psyche*, where he tells of a dream a client had after making a suicide attempt. In the dream, the client is back in the hospital ward, but has become a child again, and is in the ward to start life over from the beginning. To revert to childhood, as this client does symbolically in the dream, means to return to the innocent, undifferentiated state of the prima materia, Edinger says.[4] This reversion is a prerequisite for transformation. The dream thus signifies the psychological meaning of the suicide attempt.

The desire to end one's life may in fact reveal a need for some kind of transformation that is mistakenly believed possible after one kills themself. Addressing the decision to end one's life in a conscious way, after consulting the Self rather than out of some need of the ego, distinguishes one kind of suicide from another.

As previously mentioned, the core longing of those who attempt suicide, although often unconscious, is in fact for transformation—for a kind of death and rebirth, which the person mistakenly believes will be possible only if he or she physically kills themself. The antidote is to address this urge for transformation consciously, consulting the Self rather than some need of the ego, and to see the desire for death and rebirth as *symbolic*. We may ask what aspect of the person's current life, or self-concept, needs to "die"—to be let go of, in order to release new energy affording the strength and enthusiasm to move forward. If transformation can be achieved psychically, it may not need to be lived out literally. For the transformation to occur, a person must address the darker, destructive shadow elements of their personality, which involves dissolving the fixed, rigid, static aspects of the personality that are one sided, and have a crippling effect on spiritual and psychological growth. Such change may happen either through analysis, or through some kind of conversion experience, which involves deep and profound self-reflection.

I experienced the transformation process in my own analysis. Although I survived my encounter with the death forces while attempting suicide, those forces remained with me for more than a decade, and haunted me with their seductive call. Before I could begin to heal, I first had to acknowledge and accept the grip of these forces. I could then explore how they got constellated, and later activated. This involved a long process of excavating my early childhood traumas and their effect on me. I discovered the existence of several other complexes as well, and came to understand the many defenses I'd developed to ward off future pain. I explored my deep shame, and my enduring puella qualities, that entrapped me in a naive, and overly romantic, view of life. Because I was so identified with my puella needs, I could not yet make the adjustment to a more mature attitude— one that embraces suffering and loss, failure, and deprivation. Suffering in life is inevitable, but with maturity and wisdom we can find *meaning* in the suffering; together they can serve as kindling for an inner fire and desire to live life fully. Only then is true transformation possible.

In alchemy, fire is central to the process of transformation. *Calcinatio*, an alchemical process, which means: "going through the fire," involves the death of the ruling principle of consciousness—or the ego. The desirousness of the ego must be metaphorically consumed by fire during this process. Psychologically, this means tamping down desirousness for power, a common shadow quality which often reigns over the ego, causing one to seek control over self and others rather than operating out of love and acceptance.

In his book, *Living Between Worlds: Finding Personal Resilience in Changing Times,* James Hollis points out that in all life passages, something must die: "naivete, the old road map, a plan, an expectation, a strategy, a story."[5] The period between unconsciousness and conscious awareness can be thought of as the space in-between. We can image this as the time before the chrysalis becomes a butterfly. There is one consistency in all of nature, including our own—that "nature evolves by way of death," says Hollis.[6]

Transformation in Myths

The process of transformation is portrayed in many myths and fairytales. One of the first sources I came upon during my healing process was Estés' book, *Women Who Run with the Wolves*. She reveals the truth of being, and the ways in which we become defeated, deflated, and disempowered. Each story in her book offers a way out of depression, hopelessness, and death.

One story from Estés' book, "The Handless Maiden," tells of a young woman whose hands are chopped off by the devil with her father's permission. The father has made a pact with the devil, and the devil returns to make good on his bargain. As Estés says, "A woman's initiation begins with the poor bargain she made long ago while still slumbering."[7] It is helpful here to note that, according to Jung, all characters in dreams, and folk tales, can be seen as part of the protagonist's psyche. Hence, even though it was the young woman's *father*, who ostensibly made the pact with the devil, it was *she herself* who made that poor bargain. By saying so, Estés means a woman's unconscious willingness to give up her sense of self, her creativity, her imagination, and her instinctual life, to become what others want her to be for the sake of love, acceptance, and all that goes with it. This is the essence of the puella.

The story describes a long, painful journey that ends with the maiden discovering her true self, and being able to grow new, authentic hands. The hands regrow in stages, beginning with an understanding of all that has happened to her, and eventually to "a deep grasp of the non-concrete, the metaphoric, the sacred path she has been on."[8] Estés notes that for many women "the transformation from feeling oneself swept away or enslaved by every idea or person who raps on her door to being a woman shining with La Destina, possessed of a deep sense of her own destiny, is a miraculous one."[9]

"The Handless Maiden" resonated deeply with me. As indicated in the writing of my own story, I had made many "bad bargains." I was misled by my own, weak inner father, and sold my potential for the promise of love.

During my individuation journey, I read many stories of women (and some men), who had been on a similar path. I read about Inanna, the ancient goddess who made a descent into the underworld, where she was ripped apart, but later returned to the upper world renewed and empowered. I read the Greek myth of Persephone, who was abducted by Hades to the underworld where she was raped, and made consort to the devil himself, until she was rescued by the gods at the begging of her mother, Demeter. I read the story of Psyche, who was separated from her beloved Amour, and was required to undertake numerous difficult tasks before she could be reunited with him. Symbolically, this means reunification, or integration, of a more positive animus.

Stories such as these helped me understand the poor bargains I had made in relationships with men, and why. They have been integral to my own development, and I have passed them onto others who have made similar poor bargains, and been taken over by the Death archetype. The images in them are symbolic, which affirmed for me that the process of transformation and individuation is possible without literal death. Each story described a long, treacherous, and demanding journey of death and rebirth.

11

A CLINICAL PERSPECTIVE
Two Cases of Suicide

*As therapists, our job is to contain the opposites
and help our clients explore the depths of their
will to live, as well as their will to die, and to
hope for transformation and rebirth.*
—Christi Taylor-Jones

I describe my work with two clients in this chapter, both of whom encountered the Death archetype, and were forced to wrestle with it. Their stories are now part of my story, as I wrestled right along with them.

Charlie

Charlie (not his real name) told me he had called several therapists before me. It was my *voice*, he said, that prompted him to make the appointment. My voice had a comforting quality. In our first session, I asked him what he hoped to gain from our work together. "To feel more at peace with myself," he told me.

He said that his grandmother had died recently. She was the only person who had ever loved him. His mother had passed away three months before he first saw me, but he had hated her. Also, his girlfriend had left him after a several-year relationship, and his dog had died. He described a lifetime of abandonments, one after another. His father had left when he was a year old, and his mother had given him over to his grandmother when he was five. He felt cut off from his sisters, who had remained with his mom, and he had a brother-in-law, who he both hated and feared. Charlie said that he carried a loaded gun to protect himself, just in case.

Charlie was able to carry a gun because he worked as a security guard after failing the test to become a police officer, his dream career. He'd been referred to special education for learning disabilities as a child, and had no college education. He'd been teased a lot in school, and had few friends, although he did have one "best" friend. He said that it was hard for him to get close to anyone. One friend that he liked had committed suicide. All of these facts about Charlie's life raised red flags of concern for me.

Charlie described his life as one continuous thread of disappointments and loss. His mother was married at least twice before giving birth to him, and afterward, had many lovers. According to Charlie, his mother never wanted him, and never liked him. In fact, she wished he had never been born. Although Charlie told me, I drew this conclusion myself from the shaming comments his mother made to him. She actually didn't like men, as it turned out, even though she kept marrying them. She preferred her daughters. Charlie could do nothing right, according to his mother. His grandmother had been his only support, but in time, I realized that she, too, had lacked the necessary qualities to adequately mother Charlie. His grandmother was controlling, and feared being left alone if one of Charlie's relationships worked out. Charlie was in his forties, had never been married, and had no children. He was more or less a loner.

During our work together, I suggested to Charlie that he sign up with the Big Brothers program, or another organization that would enable him to mentor someone. I felt that there was something of a "failed hero" in him, which manifested in his desire to be a cop, and protect people from the "bad guys." It also led to his subsequent career in security. He seemed to like kids, at least in the abstract. I thought that mentoring would help build Charlie's self-esteem, and give his life more meaning—to mentor a young boy, since he might never have a son of his own. He never followed through.

Charlie drank heavily before entering therapy. He came from a long line of alcoholics, but he somehow managed to stop. I saw this as a strength. Charlie admitted that he thought about suicide occasionally; however, he wasn't suicidal at the time. He was instead, filled with rage—a condition that continued throughout our time together. Charlie projected his anger onto others, which gave rise to almost paranoid fantasies about people doing violence to him, or to others. He knew how to play the shame-and-blame game.

Charlie's fantasies about killing bad guys as a cop underscored his desire to be a hero. He was always wanting to save someone—a person or an animal, from an evil *other*. I wondered if there was a way to redirect these energies toward a more constructive purpose. Charlie's emotions manifested in the extreme—both love and loyalty, as well as hate and vengefulness. He either felt deeply about things, or was numb to them. One thing that Charlie was numb to was any positive feeling for his mother. On the other hand, he claimed to love his grandmother dearly, in whom he saw no flaws, despite the fact that she seemed controlling. He was unable to hold the tension of opposites, in any form, for the purpose of integrating them.

He often used the word: *kill* when talking about his anger, and what he would like to do to someone who was evil. Ironically, I thought deep down that Charlie believed that *he* himself was evil. This potential realization must have been so overpowering that Charlie had to project much of the evilness outside of himself. He said that he wasn't afraid of death, although he did not believe in a benevolent god, so I wondered what he thought he'd encounter in the next life. Would it be more of the same, or the sweet comfort of nothingness? He said that he didn't think about it.

We talked a lot about Charlie's angry feelings, and how to manage them. We discussed black-and-white thinking, and how to avoid it; we talked about relationships with women and how to find his "softer self," how to get his needs met in constructive ways, and how to reframe his catastrophizing thoughts and be good to himself. I identified ways in which I thought that he was scapegoated in his family, and how it seemed that many of the family's "shadow" aspects got projected onto him. I suggested that he had internalized all of this negativity and shame. I told him that I wanted us to rewrite his story based on an understanding of his past, with a belief in a different story going forward.

A Clinical Perspective

Christmas was approaching. Charlie had no plans for the holidays, but he gave me a hundred-dollar gift certificate to a restaurant that he liked. I explained to him that I could not accept the gift, and asked instead for him to express what I meant to him. What was the message in the money? I had clearly constellated the Savior archetype for him. What the money represented was his gratitude for all of my help. I embodied everything good and kind in his world. I knew that it was his first Christmas without his grandmother, and suggested that he find someone with whom to spend the holidays. I told him how touched I was by his generosity, something I hoped that he would show to more people in his personal life.

Money is often symbolic of emotional and psychological resources, something of which Charlie was in great need. Instead of accessing those resources within himself, he sought to give them away. Maybe, he felt that I was his best resource for healing, or he secretly, and metaphorically, wished that he were going to the restaurant with me—that he could make union with me in a way that was nourishing to him. These interpretations didn't occur to me until later. I just knew that Charlie was trying to do something generous and kind, and I wondered if he felt rejected by my not accepting his gift.

That New Years, Charlie called a suicide hotline. He did not tell me so until the following week. He said he didn't feel he had any purpose in life. Soon afterward, I encouraged Charlie to turn over his guns to his best friend, whom I had also asked to keep watch on Charlie for the next couple of weeks. His friend agreed, and Charlie didn't fight my request. I asked Charlie to call me each day—to check in, at which time I would determine whether he needed to come in for a session before our next appointment. I also consulted Charlie's psychiatrist about the medications that he was taking, and whether, or not, they were working. I informed the psychiatrist that Charlie seemed barely able to hold his life together. Charlie was depressed over work, his grandmother, his sister, and his ex-girlfriend. He was vomiting from stress, and needed to be tested for an ulcer. The doctor completely agreed with me.

Charlie journaled as best he could. He did all of the homework assignments that I gave him, like a good little student. He read the books on grief that I gave him. He thought about dating again, and even about applying to community college. Charlie told me about a dream that he had, which was about having sex with his niece, with whom he had a positive relationship. I interpreted this to mean that he was wanting a more positive union with the Feminine, with the more "feeling side" of himself. I saw his niece as a positive anima figure (the female side of a man). Charlie later dreamed about "running out of ammo," which seemed to represent his not being able to protect himself, feeling vulnerable to hurt. Ammunition seemed a violent way of protecting himself, though, and we discussed whether he might find other ways to protect himself. "Running out of ammo" might also have meant that he was running out of fight, resigning, giving up. I was glad that I took the initiative previously to have Charlie's guns removed from his possession.

Two events happened in the ensuring months that caused Charlie much distress: Charlie learned that his ex-girlfriend got married. He also heard rumors about the company he worked for that suggested to him that he might lose his job. He said that the company was in danger of being sold. Meanwhile, he was experiencing memory problems, which the doctor told him could be the result of his antidepressants. The doctor was going to test Charlie for possible dementia.

Charlie said that if he was diagnosed with dementia, he'd kill himself. "I don't want to end up in a sanatorium," he told me. I assured Charlie that he wouldn't end up in a sanatorium. I saw no indication of dementia. I also told him that maybe I was pushing him too hard, and was not sensitive enough to his struggles. Maybe, my insensitivity added to his stress. He said no, that I was helping him.

The test results showed no sign of dementia. The doctor said that Charlie's memory problems stemmed from stress and depression. Charlie continued taking the antidepressants. He talked about moving to Las Vegas, and starting over. The anniversary of Charlie's grandmother's death was soon upon him as well, causing him to spiral downward again. He'd always felt guilty that he hadn't done more to keep her alive. He was also angry at her doctors and nurses.

After Charlie's grandmother died, he tried to keep his mother from attending the funeral. His mother and grandmother often fought. We talked about forgiveness, and what he'd need to forgive his mother for, and himself. Charlie said that his mother slapped him whenever he cried as a child, so he did not cry for her when she died. Charlie had turned all his grief into anger, I told him, because anger is a more powerful emotion than sadness. For the first time, he cried during his therapy session, and afterward, he hugged me. This would be the only time that I would see such an outpouring of feeling from Charlie.

We continued to work on Charlie's grief. He remained stuck in two stages of grief: bargaining and anger. Eventually, Charlie could sense sadness around his mother's passing, as well as for all of the other losses that he'd experienced, which I saw as an encouraging sign. He started seeing his best friend again, and contacting other friends, too. Charlie's life was on the upswing.

As Christmas neared again, Charlie felt better than he had in a while. He said he was tired of making the long drive to see me, and that he wanted a referral to someone closer to his home. He said that he was grateful for all of my help, and that he was "feeling much better." We discussed Charlie's decision to discontinue my therapy services at length. He insisted that the drive from his home to my office was too much of a hardship, and that traffic was getting worse. I wondered if I had let Charlie down in some way, or if the work was too intense for him. Although we had made progress, he seemed limited in his ability to work in any depth. I finally accepted his reason, and right, to leave as valid, and that while the work was not finished, he would continue therapy with someone else. I set to work on finding an appropriate referral.

At our last session, just before Christmas, Charlie gifted me with a jar of Vermont honey, symbolic of the sweetness and goodness he seemed to project onto me. He apparently held onto the sourness for himself, because two weeks later, on New Years Eve, Charlie shot himself with one of the guns that his friend had been holding for him. Apparently, Charlie told his friend, with whom I later spoke, that he was feeling much better now, so the friend had returned the guns. I found out about Charlie's death a couple months after he died; someone called me, who had found my name and number in Charlie's wallet. I was devastated to the core, especially because I felt that I had failed to save him, even after managing to save myself years before. I knew I would spend the rest of my professional life contemplating the difference, and wondering if I could have done more.

Since then, I've become more attuned to the possibility of suicidal feelings in the clients whom I treat. I recognize that each person has their own story about life and death, and that ultimately, the individual psyche, and our relationship to it, determines our fate.

When Charlie terminated his therapy sessions with me, he was already determined to end his life. He never contacted the referrals that I gave him. He immediately asked his friend to return his guns, and like so many people who begin their emergence from depression, Charlie now had the energy to carry out his mission of self-destruction, leaving behind the symbolic honey, or sweetness, he couldn't use. Ironically, a year before Charlie's death, also during the Christmas holiday, he had called the suicide hotline. Christmas, as we know, is a symbolic day—a time when the "savior" was born, only to be crucified later. Christmas marks the end of one year, and the beginning of a new year—thus, a time of death and rebirth.

The symbolism of honey is also instructive, as Charlie both gave, and left behind, honey—at least symbolically. Edward Edinger talks about individuation in alchemical terms; he describes psychological dynamics in terms of specific operations. One such operation is called: *coagulatio*, which in alchemy means: the state in which things become solidified, made solid. In psychological terms, *coagulatio* refers to a solidifying of the ego, or personality. As Edinger states, "Coagulatio is promoted by action. . . . Psychologically, this means that activity and psychic movement promote ego development."[1]

An agent of coagulatio is lead, associated with Saturn, which is heavy and burdensome. Psychologically, lead represents states of depression, melancholy, and limitation, that must be overcome. Edinger points out, "In analytic practice this linkage with lead is often accomplished when the individual takes personal responsibility for fleeting fantasies and ideas by expressing them to the analyst or to another significant person."[2]

Another agent of coagulatio is sulfur, which manifests in desire. According to Jung, sulfur "is the active substance of the sun or, in psychological language, the motive factor in consciousness"; on the other hand, sulfur also symbolizes compulsion, "an involuntary motivation or impulse ranging from mere interest to possession proper."[3] Thus, sulfur is paradoxical, both an element of life-giving warmth, and the stink and blackness of hell.

Edinger also states that "if part of the meaning of Sulphur is desirousness—the stiving for power and pleasure—we reach the conclusion that desire coagulates" and desire initiates the incarnation process.[4] "Without that desire there would be nothing but eternal stillness without substantiality," he says.[5] Edinger claims that coagulation is not needed for people who are already driven by desire, but those without adequate libido investment (meaning desire) need "to cultivate their desires—(to) seek them, nourish them, and act on them."[6] This was something that Charlie was unable to do.

Edinger also points out that honey is the supreme example of sweetness, is related to desire, and that the famous alchemist, Gerhard Dorn, claimed that the recipe for joining body and spirit requires honey.[7] Jung, however, pointed out that the "sweetness of the earth [is] not without its dangers, for the honey could

A Clinical Perspective

change into a deadly poison.... it contains 'Tartarum', which has to do with Hades."[8] That is, honey may also be psychologically associated with hell and evil. Tartarum is also associated with Saturn. According to Edinger, alchemist, Jacob Boehm, claimed that "Saturn hath in its power the chamber of death and is a drier up of all powers from whence corporeity existeth."[9]

In other words, each alchemical operation, like each stage of individuation, carries within it elements that can cause forward movement, or cause to completely dissolve—such as the personality in the individuation process. According to Edinger, "Exposing oneself to the storm and stress of action, the churn of reality, solidifies the personality."[10] At the same time, these storms and stresses can activate a regression, or overattachment to the objects of desire in which the person becomes lost and self-destructive. We see this with alcohol and drug addiction.

In analysis, a positive-transference relationship can usher in the beginning of coagulatio, as it activates desire. This is the stage at which I thought Charlie and myself were at when he decided to change therapists. The fact that Charlie left me with the symbolic honey and sweetness could suggest a sign of some forward movement toward ego development. However, the poisonous attachment to negative feelings, and his inability to hold onto the sweetness for himself, blocked his further progress.

At the close of our last session, Charlie asked me if his situation, and our work together, would help me in working with other people like him. An odd question.

I said, "Yes, I learn from everyone whom I treat. Sometimes, I get more from them than they get from me." In the case of Charlie, I got both more, and less. I did not get the result that I was seeking, but that was never entirely up to me. What I did get, was a deeper understanding of my abilities, and limitations, as a therapist. I also gleaned more insight into the experience of someone dead set on suicide.

Looking back, to enumerate Charlie's risk factors is not difficult. There was, for example his early emotional neglect and abuse. No "mothering function" existed in his psyche to nurture and help cultivate a sense of self. Charlie also suffered from learning disabilities, and was bullied and made fun of. He had problems with self-regulation, was fairly isolated, had few friends or love relationships, suffered several losses, owned guns, exhibited both shame and rage, and tended to blame others as a defense against his own sense of worthlessness. He was unable to hold, or integrate, any pair of opposites (love/hate, good/bad, smart/dumb, etc.). He saw everything in black and white, and felt hopeless about the future. Charlie enjoyed little, and looked forward to even less. All of his feelings were long standing. In addition, Charlie lacked the psychological depth, curiosity, and resilience that someone else with his problems might have—and that might have saved his life.

Charlie's problems, like those of my brother, were chronic. Therapy offered some hope that things would improve. I believe what finally put Charlie over the edge was a series of events and conditions that shattered all hope: the marriage to someone else of the only woman he loved—a woman who, in his mind, had offered him his last chance for relationship; the threat of losing his job and the possibility that he wouldn't be able to get another one; fears, despite what the doctors said, that he really did have some form of dementia and would lose his mind entirely; and finally, that if any of these events or conditions disabled him, he would be alone, lacking the physical and emotional supports that he needed to survive.

    This, of course, is all conjecture. What I do know, is that acute problems were heaped onto chronic problems, and that Charlie lacked the inner or outer resources to care for himself, or to find meaning in his circumstances. It is my belief, that Charlie had reached the end, and knew of no other way to start anew except through death. In this way, his suicide reflected a longing for rebirth.

Sandy

Years after Charlie's death, and after working with many other clients who expressed suicidal feelings, I developed a better understanding of the suicidal impulse. I also had a clearer understanding of the events and feelings leading up to my own suicide attempt. I became more confident in treating clients who were suicidal, or had suicidal thoughts. Ethical judgments tended to override legal concerns about how and when to intervene—something I feel is necessary in working with suicidal clients. The client's feelings deserve respect and validation, rather than being pathologized. My primary focus was on the psyche, and especially the messages from the Self.

    Of the many clients that I treated, no one had more reason to kill herself than Sandy. She entered therapy with an almost unbelievable story of emotional and physical trauma that had led to a lifelong dissociation of feeling and memory. Sandy's story began with a near-death experience when she was a small child. Whether she fell, or was pushed from a five-story building, remains unclear; however, she had clearly been playing next to the window when her fall happened. She was four years old. The fact that Sandy survived was miraculous. She was living in a foreign country at the time, but soon afterward the family immigrated to the United States of America. Sandy and her family had lived in three different countries before finally arriving in the United States.

A few years later, Sandy happened to notice a large scar on the back of her arm, which she asked her older brother about. He informed her that she had fallen out the bedroom window of their apartment, intimating that the incident was somehow her fault. Sandy's brother told her to not talk about the scar or her fall out the window with their parents, as the conversation would just upset them. He added that she had already put them through enough suffering.

Sandy could only recall vague memories of the accident, the surgery it entailed, and what happened afterward. For some time, Sandy suffered from severe migraines that caused hallucinations. She had hit the ground so hard when she fell as a child, that her brain had swollen, and left her in a coma for three days. Aside from migraines and hallucinations, afterward she also experienced depression and high fever.

Sandy's parents had ignored these symptoms, other than to put ice on her head, or bathe her in ice water; they did not take her to the hospital. When they finally *did* take her to a doctor, the source of Sandy's migraines could not be identified, although the cause was assumed to be due to the accident. Doctors also said that Sandy had Hepatitis C, probably from the surgery, although nearly undetectable by now. The doctors concluded that there was nothing to be done for Sandy at this point. Yet, the headaches continued, which were so severe that Sandy wished that she could die. She had no idea what was wrong with her, but clearly her suffering wasn't normal. Although Sandy's suffering continued, she stopped telling anyone about it.

Sandy's immigrant parents worked long hours, often holding down two or more jobs, which left Sandy alone, or in the care of her brother, who either verbally abused her, or ignored her and left her to care for herself. She began to have thoughts of suicide.

At fourteen, Sandy dated an older student who raped her, and threatened to hurt her, or her family, if she broke up with him. She attended a mostly white school, where she was one of a few Asians, and had no support system. Not only did other kids bully Sandy, but the police did as well; they frequently stopped her to check for possible drugs, rather than protect her from her tormentors. She did not tell anyone about the rape, or threats on her life.

Finally, at a Bible camp one year, Sandy confided in a friend. He, and another friend, took Sandy to the camp minister, who convinced her to report the rape to the police. Buoyed by both the minster's and her friend's support, she did just that. A few weeks later, her boyfriend sent a couple of guys to her house, tied up her mother and brother, and threatened to kill them all. It was a staged home invasion, and a few people at school knew who sent the invaders. Yet, no one said a word. Her family tried to forget about the incident. Sandy blamed herself, and wished that she had not gone to the police, who hadn't followed up with an investigation anyway, and nothing happened to those who had terrorized her.

By this time, Sandy was a teenager, and obsessed with planning her own death; she researched different suicide methods, and considered the pros and cons of each one. Among other things, she considered starving herself and, in fact, reduced her food intake to almost nothing. Nearly starving herself gave Sandy some sense of control. She relished her ability not to give in to hunger. She even drank bleach, nail polish remover, and hydrogen peroxide, and swallowed almost an entire bottle of Motrin. She considered jumping off a building, or smashing her car, or slitting her wrists with a razor blade. She decided against any method that would involve intense physical pain, or leave a mess for someone else to clean up. She felt that God would forgive her for killing herself because she suffered so much from the migraines, hallucinations, and insomnia—from which she got no relief. The Hepatitis C caused stomach cramps, sweating, fevers, chills, body aches, weakness, and dizziness, which resulted in her collapsing at one point. Sandy's biggest fear, though, was that she would survive any suicide attempt. She felt completely invisible.

Starting at age twelve, several times Sandy attempted to run away, but was always brought back home. She had become the scapegoat of the family, while her brother took on the role of family hero. To her parents, he could do no wrong. Although unsafe in the world, Sandy never attributed her predicament to anyone but herself. She suffered from deep, unconscious shame. She felt that any pain that she suffered was her fault.

She began taking drugs in late adolescence. When Sandy was old enough to leave home, she moved to New York, where she became a heroin addict. Sandy's life grew very dark. At one point, her best friend committed suicide. Sandy and her friend had made a suicide pact, but Sandy couldn't go through with it. She tried to convince him not to either, but he did.

A Clinical Perspective

After her friend's death, Sandy tried to get sober. She told of going to a hospital in New York City and sitting on a bench for hours as she waited to be admitted. She was sick, sweating, and unable even to sit up, when a police officer approached the hospital staff, and inquired about her. He said that he'd been on patrol all night, and that every time he came by the bench, he saw her slumped in agony. He wondered why she had not been tended to. The nurses told him that she'd often come here, that she was an addict, and there was no point in helping her—she'd just be back the next day. The officer demanded that the hospital staff attend to Sandy; he insisted that he would not relent until they did.

Finally, the hospital admitted Sandy. She was taken to a detox room, where a black woman came up to her, looked her square in the eyes, and asked, "What are YOU doing in here? You don't belong here!"

Sandy said that she did belong, that she was an addict.

The woman said, "No, you don't belong here. You're going to beat this. I can see that you have angels all around you, and they won't let you give up, so you better stop trying!"

Sandy relayed the story with humility, and with gratitude for this woman, who was one of her angels, as was the police officer. I could immediately relate to her story. She got sober afterward, and moved to Los Angeles, where she committed herself to a career as an artist, something for which she had a tremendous, but unrealized, gift.

When I met Sandy a few years later, she was afraid to tell me her story. It was parceled out in pieces over many years. She initially feared that I would think that she was crazy, and put her in a mental institution, especially when she told me of the hallucinations and visions that she experienced as a child. That never occurred to me. Sandy was a petite and attractive young woman with enormous creative potential. She was also bright and insightful—and even wise, which surprised me, given all that she had been through.

While I was seeing Sandy, she became involved with a man, who was controlling and possessive. She was beginning to enjoy some real success as an artist, which threatened him. In addition, he knew that she was independently wealthy—at least modestly so, because during Sandy's adolescence, her parents opened a successful business, and became quite affluent. Perhaps, her boyfriend saw her as his meal ticket. Having known so little love in her life, Sandy became convinced that the reason he wanted to spend so much time with her was because he loved her. In reality, he kept her captive, rejecting her friends, and even encouraging her to stop seeing me.

Eventually, she decided to end the relationship, but as with her boyfriend when she was fourteen, she suffered the consequences. For months, the man that she broke up with stalked her, damaged her house, and almost set it on fire. She became the victim of gaslighting to the point that she didn't know what was real, and what was not. It took enormous strength and courage for Sandy to manage the daily and nightly fears that he would find her.

In desperation, Sandy sold her house and moved away, but she continued to live in fear for the next few years, and became a virtual recluse. The fear itself became a problem. She could not practice as an artist. She could not appear at openings, or shows, or in any way have a public presence. In addition to analysis, we agreed that maybe some eye movement desensitization reprocessing (EMDR) would help. It did, and between the two therapies, her fear lessened over time, and she

A Clinical Perspective

was eventually able to begin exploring what had happened to her in her relationship as well as in her life with her family.

After more than a decade of analysis and other therapies, Sandy was able to unravel the dark, diabolical events that led to her deep shame and self-destructive tendencies, including her reenactments with possessive, and violent, men. She was able to reclaim the small child inside her, and to grow into her wise, talented, and powerful feminine self. After several years, she was even able to resurrect her career as an artist.

In contrast to Charlie, Sandy carried within her a hidden fire that fueled her curiosity and creativity. She had an incredible resilience that awed me to the core. Her fall from the window accident led to a near-death experience, which she remembered as entering a lighted tunnel. After that experience, she did not fear death. In fact, she seemed, as she said, "addicted to death." Yet, Sandy did not take her life. She was determined to live her life to its fullest. As a child, she drew, which she said gave her a sense of worth, knowing she did something well. Despite her diminutive size, she was physically strong, and able to do the work of two men, as I witnessed when she worked on a room-sized sculpture that required cutting, welding, carrying large pieces of wood, and setting up her art installations. She also packed wall-sized paintings, and other works of art, into her truck. Most of all, Sandy never shied away from looking at herself with clear eyes, always willing to explore her psychological depths, regardless of any anxiety and sadness that such an exploration sometimes prompts.

Edward Edinger says, "Courage means a willingness to face anxiety. Continuous regime means that through all shifts of mood and mental states one is willing to persevere in the effort to scrutinize and understand what is happening."[11] Sandy had immense courage in that she lived with overwhelming, almost paralyzing, fear. She lacked support through some of the hardest times of her life, and failed to recognize support when it was truly there for her—a perspective came only in retrospect. Her family's attitude toward her was one of indifference, contempt, and dismissiveness, as was true of many of her friends—reenactments of judgment that convinced her that there must be something wrong with her.

Sandy's breakthroughs came in spurts. She even stopped therapy for a while. Once, she went to Europe for several months to gain some distance and clarity. But she always returned when she felt that she could not completely heal on her own. I would like to claim Sandy as my success story, to believe that I had some part in her healing journey; the truth is, that Sandy entered this life with a quality that enabled her to endure incredible suffering. Perhaps each obstacle she overcame further infused her with a certain determination, or maybe her coming so close to death so early in life convinced her to stay in it for as long as she could. Having a way to express herself artistically may have protected her from a kind of implosion. Her ability to survive, however, had nothing to do with intelligence or wealth. During most of her childhood, she had lived in poverty. Her parents were immigrants. She was not welcomed into the world by any of the countries she inhabited, including the United States.

After Sandy moved to a new house, she also found a new partner—a large, beautiful pup, who is her constant companion. She has returned to her art, and has continued the journey of individuation.

12

SUMMARY AND REFLECTIONS

The goal of life is not happiness but meaning.
—James Hollis

This book has focused primarily on the psychology of suicide from the point of view of those who have attempted, or seriously considered, killing themselves. However, a third group of people exists, who are touched by suicide—the ones left behind. This group includes the many individuals who have lost a loved one to suicide. Words such as *shame, dissociation, guilt,* and *chronic sorrow* are among the feeling reactions that these people describe.[1] Many survivors of suicide remain traumatized and suffer long-standing grief. Some of the surviving members have ancestors who committed suicide; the legacies of those ancestors were handed down through the generations, and still have an impact. I have not focused on survivors of suicide because much has been written about them.

In contrast, little has been written about or by those who have attempted suicide and have lived to tell about it "from the inside." Some of those individuals have previously experienced, and grieved the loss of someone who committed suicide before their own failed attempt. For those people, the questions that linger are: Why them and not me? Why did I survive? In this book, I have attempted to shed some light on why such people survived. However, my answers are inconclusive, and beg for more research.

I have heard people say that those who survive suicide are more resilient, but my experience indicates that truly resilient people are less likely to attempt suicide in the first place. Yet, there is a kind of resilience that can reveal itself after one has made the attempt. This suggests that the suicide attempt erupted from a desire to find redemption and transformation. After the attempt, such people may feel as if they still have something to learn, that their purpose has not yet been fulfilled.

For a long time, I could not bring myself to tell even my closest friends that I had once tried to kill myself, much less that my suicidal feelings had not fully abated. Suicidal thoughts continued to plague me off and on for years. I feared that my transparency about the issue would drastically change the way people saw me—that, despite what people said, they would judge me as inherently flawed, mentally ill, or just weak. I even feared that I might prove them right, and make another attempt. Then they could say, "I knew it! She was always emotionally fragile." That fear lessened as I began to understand what drove me, and others, to suicide. My fear diminished as I listened to the stories and feelings of clients, friends, and family members who felt as I did. I now realize how pervasive the death wish is in many people and how it can get activated, even in people one would never expect to entertain such a thought.

Summary and Reflections

Throughout this writing, I have talked about the Death archetype that, when constellated, can pull one toward death. Freud called this archetype *Thanatos*, or the death instinct, named for the god of death in ancient Greek mythology. The death archetype is described by various experts as a kind of inner saboteur, or adviser, who tries to convince the suicidal person to kill him- or herself.[2] In Jungian terms, we might call this a "negative animus/anima," or even a "death complex." Michael Sinason talks about a "cohabitation," or pairing, of Eros and Thanatos (life and death) within the psyche.[3] It is almost as if the psyche contains two separate personalities. Commenting on Sinason's work, Robert M. Young says, "Sinason maintains that mental illness is ubiquitous, that we are each and all a body with two (and only two) minds. The second personality is not a repository of trauma. It is hard wired and cannot learn. . . . [Sinason] holds that a full-blooded other, a whole personality, cohabits with the 'I' personality, with all *its* range of abilities, feelings and irrationalities."[4]

In Jungian psychology, we might think of this other personality as a kind of shadow part of the psyche. Joscelyn Richards describes a dream of one of her schizophrenic clients, who was besieged by inner voices urging him to kill himself.[5] In reading the dream, that Richards reported, I was struck by how powerful this voice could be. I realized, too, that one need not be psychotic to hear such a voice. It's the call of death from the psyche, even if that voice makes no sound at all. As W. H. Auden says, "We are lived by powers we pretend to understand."[6]

One of Richards's clients dreamed that two people were walking alongside a railroad track: one had the impulse to jump onto the track to his death, while the other sought to rescue the jumper. The dream aptly describes the two forces in the psyche, one that seeks life, the other that seeks death. If one is lucky, as was the dreamer in Richards's article, and in my own life, there is someone willing and able to listen to both voices, and to bring consciousness and meaning to bare. Sadly, that is not the case for everyone. For some, no outer voice emerges to speak to the inner voice of death, and so the death voice takes hold. Perhaps the person who dies is unable, or unwilling, to be rescued.

Marion Woodman, in her book *The Pregnant Virgin*, describes an inner figure that she calls "the demon lover," who is constellated in a woman's psyche when she is "cut off inwardly from her positive masculine guide," and identifies with the "dark side of the father archetype." Says Woodman, "There is no one to mediate between her terrorized ego and the chaos through which it is falling. The abyss is bottomless. . . . She has done everything to make herself acceptable and she has failed; she is unlovable and that verdict resonates right back to the primary abandonment. . . . Suicide in that situation may become a fulfillment of her destiny." In such a case, says Woodman, "Suicide is a final stroke of vengeance against the savage god who has abandoned her."[1]

This idea of an "inner Other" is pervasive in the literature. Olga Mikhailova approaches suicide as a "personal drama." She says that "the Other is always with us and inside us with the full destructive power of its gaze."[8] At any time, this "Other" can take over, as Jung first observed. The reasons are varied.

Herbert Hendin points out, "The meanings of suicide are often unconscious and then best elicited by free associations and dreams."[9] He quotes a 1970 study by David L. Raphling, which finds that two-thirds (60 percent) of suicidal patients

Summary and Reflections

in one study remembered dreams from the period just prior to their suicide attempt. With the exception of six patients, dreams occurred during a time when the subjects were preoccupied with suicidal thoughts. In comparison with the control group, the thematic content of the dreams of suicidal individuals included explicit references to actual or threatened death or dead persons and revealed acts of violence or destruction.[10] Says Hendin, "Eliciting the dreams of suicidal patients is an important part of a psychiatric evaluation."[11] He tells of a patient of his own who jumped in front of a train in an attempt to kill herself—similar to that of Richards's client. She lost both legs but lived to tell of the following dream: "She was in a long, narrow tunnel and could see a light at the end of it. She walked toward the light and there she saw a man and a woman standing over a manger."[12]

A tunnel in dreams often represents the birth process, something I've observed in many patients seeking rebirth. The dreamer's father in this case had abandoned her mother, and the dreamer, when she was nine years old, so the dream suggests a rejoining of mother, father, and client. The manger, of course, reminds us of Christ's birth, so the elements of death and rebirth seem clear. Hendin says, "She (the client) saw her life as set on a course in which gratification of her fantasies was only possible through her death."[13]

Unfortunately, I do not recall any dreams prior to, or immediately after, my own suicide attempt, but, years later, after my mother's death, I had a dream in which she was painting for me a beautiful butterfly in more complete form than I had ever imagined. In the dream she said, "I can't draw butterflies like I used to."

I wrote about the dream in an article for *Psychological Perspectives*.[14] In it, I interpreted the message to be of reconnecting, not just to my biological mother, but to a spiritual mother as well, a kind of Great Mother that awaited me—and perhaps my own mother, beyond death. I now see my dream as a prophetic, transformational dream about my own life going forward, since soon afterward, I entered Jungian analysis, and began my rebirth journey in this life. Mikhailova notes that "the most common state of mind in suicide finds its most striking expression in one's sincere desire to die and an equally strong desire to live."[15]

While one must respect the negative, death-dealing aspects of the psyche, all this suggests that the psyche is ultimately ambivalent about whether to continue to live, or to die, literally *and* symbolically. One person, whom I talked to for this book, described a lifelong battle with the pull to death. He explained that the state of the world, and his position in it, makes it hard for him not to want to die. He says that he is angry, and specifically at God, for his predicament. He has never experienced any success in his life, in his career or his relationships. Despite all his efforts, life and God have let him down. He feels that he deserves better. He also suffers from shame at not being able to do better for himself. Yet, he has not yet killed himself because he knows someone would find his body, and that would cause the person who found him much pain. So, essentially he stays alive to protect others from having to suffer his death by suicide That said, the people in his life whom he loves, and who love him, do suffer, almost constantly, from the fear that he will die, and that he will die by suicide. I think to myself how I would like for him to find meaning in the life that he still has left, as well as

Summary and Reflections

the life that he has lived; but, for now, the only meaning life has for him, except in occasional daily joys, is that he has an ability to save others from further suffering. What he has not accepted, is that life *is* suffering, and we don't always have a choice in the source, or nature, of that suffering.

I have talked about conscious suffering, and conscious choices, regarding life and death. Many people, though, carry an unconscious desire to die that gets acted out in less obvious ways, be it drug addiction, alcoholism, reckless and dangerous behavior, or other ways of provoking death, or living a slow death.

I have also touched on the conscious aspect of assisted suicide in this writing. I have described mercy killings, such as senicide and ubasute, that are carried out by some cultures in the belief that they serve the greater community, as when a person has outlived their purpose to society. I have not talked about another kind of mercy killing—that of assisting in the death of those who lack the ability to make a conscious choice to live, or to die. In this group, their brains are no longer capable of such decisions, so they linger, sometimes for years, in a kind of limbo between life and death.

Such was the case of someone I knew who cared for her mother as she descended into the underworld of Alzheimer's. The toll on both women was immense. Due to the stress of caring for her mother, my friend developed MS. The illness, in turn, cut short her own life. I have witnessed the agony of others who have watched loved ones disappear into a shadowy netherworld of cognitive decline.

Still others say they will kill themselves before they enter such a state. One can hardly blame them. Yet, while they live, the psyche lives, and one can only wonder what the Self has in mind by putting them through such a situation. It is a question with which we, as a society, must eventually deal, as medical advances have outpaced the livable lifespan. Many people may live as mere vegetables before the body finally gives out, and medical interventions can no longer keep them alive. As it now stands, there is little interest in public discourse about what to do with those who may be among the living dead. Meanwhile, survivors live with the guilt of wishing their loved one a speedy passing, knowing that he or she is beyond choice in the matter.

Finally, in order to understand the suicidal mind, one must acknowledge that for some people, there are fates worse than death—among them are: feelings of chronic shame, humiliation, despair, loneliness, grief, and persistent, severe illness, and physical and/or psychological pain. By themselves, none of these factors constitutes a diagnosis of mental illness, although a mental illness may be present. Without a diagnosis, insurance companies will not pay for treatment. Therapists carefully navigate this dilemma in order to help those who suffer, but are not mentally ill.

Sometimes mental health professionals seem more concerned with keeping the suicidal person alive, than in helping them live a life of purpose. Suicide prevention must address the matter of purpose in human suffering, while also helping people manage that suffering. I have suggested in this book that a critical aspect of this work is, first, to acknowledge and accept that suffering is a natural part of life, and, second, to develop the ability to make *meaning* out of the suffering. This effort requires holding the opposites of life and death, Eros and Thanatos, until a third transcendent function emerges to reconcile the opposites.

Summary and Reflections

In my own case, it seems that the Death archetype was always with me. Perhaps it was constellated at birth when the umbilical cord was wrapped around my neck, threatening to suffocate me. Research shows that people who have suffered from birth trauma often have difficulty with life transitions. They don't navigate change well, regardless of the type of birth trauma they endured. Sudden moves, losses, or forced changes of any kind may be met with fear and foreboding. These transitions may even be experienced as a kind of death. A palpable, physiological reaction is experienced in the body. Adjustment is arduous, as it was for me each time I moved, or lost someone important in my life, or even changed jobs or careers.

Positive changes can be as hard as dreaded ones. For some people, getting married, or receiving a promotion, can activate the Death archetype. Something is dying, even if it is for purposes of further development. At my wedding in Hawaii, I suddenly developed laryngitis, and could hardly speak my vows. I now interpret this as the psyche resisting the step that I was taking, anticipating getting married as a death. My voice returned later that night, after the wedding.

In Jane Wheelwright's book *Death of a Woman*, she shares the journey of a young woman, who is living with terminal cancer, and wanting to die. Wheelwright works with the young woman and her desire to die, while also instilling in her the value of continuing the individuation process. This, in large part, is what kept the woman from committing suicide. She lived right up to the end.[16]

A client of mine who threatened suicide whenever things went badly for her could always be talked off the ledge when I reminded her that, despite her continued narrative that everything was a disappointment, the story wasn't over. She didn't like the few chapters of her life that she had already read, but she didn't know how the story ended. I'd beseeched her to stay, and read the whole book, before making any judgment. It was my way of saying, "One day at a time." What I really meant, was that the process of individuation isn't over. Don't you want to see how far you can go?

A line from the black poet, Amir Sulaiman, conveys the idea that because someday we "will be somebody's ancestor," we need to "act accordingly."[17] That is, we need to live the message we want to hand down to our descendants, regardless of how, or when, we die. These words imply that our lives have inherent meaning beyond the living of them.

Jung claimed that neurosis "must be understood, ultimately, as the suffering of a soul which has not discovered its meaning."[18] Not only is one's life meaningful, but everything that happens in it has meaning, regardless of how painful it may feel in the moment.

As an analyst, then, I attempt not to rid my clients' lives of suffering, but rather to help them carry their suffering consciously, and to explore the possible meaning that suffering has for them. Over time, I have discovered the many layers of meaning in my own suicide attempt,. My goal is to help others do the same. I have learned that depression is a form of suffering, and a signal, that something must be addressed in one's life and psyche. Suffering signals a need for introspection, self-reflection and healing. Medication is not always the answer.

Anxiety is also a factor in suicide, one that is overlooked. Oftentimes, anxiety is a symptom of some element about to enter consciousness, an anticipation of a new awareness that

Summary and Reflections

may help enlarge the personality. Grief, too, alerts us to the need to integrate our loss, to take our time, to take care of ourselves so that we can absorb what has happened. Feelings are thus valuable sources of expanded consciousness and meaning. To deny feelings is to stay small, unformed, and unconscious. Denial of feelings limits our humanity. It diminishes our ability to feel compassion and empathy, the cornerstones of relationship with others. James Hollis put it eloquently when he said, "Avoiding dismal states of the soul becomes itself a form of suffering, for one can never relax, never let go of the frantic desire to be happy and untroubled. Rather, one is unavoidably pulled down and under, frequently painfully."[19]

All death needs to be mourned, whether it comes at our own hand, or at the hands of another, or from illness, or old age. My mother died of cancer, my father died of old age and a broken heart, my brother died of suicide. Both of my paternal grandparents died suddenly from heart attacks. Whether we die suddenly, or after years of illness and pain, we carry our suffering with us to the end, whenever that is. Each life has meaning, as does each death. We cannot know which deaths, if any, were premature in terms of their purpose, much less the longings of the soul. Apparently, when I attempted suicide, my own purpose had not yet been fully served. In many ways, it had just begun.

APPENDIX 1
The Case of Suicide in Seattle

To illustrate how distorting and confusing statistics can be, let's look at suicide rates in Seattle, Washington, a city associated with depression and suicide due to the dark, rainy weather, and lack of sunlight several months of the year. These conditions are believed to result in a form of depression known as: seasonal affective disorder (SAD). A 2020 article in the *Seattle Times* reported that Seattle was the "saddest metro area in the nation."[1] Almost half of the adults in the city reported feelings of depression, according to one survey. Ironically, Seattle was tied, in this respect, with Arizona, one of the sunniest states in the country, while the lowest reports of depression that particular month were found in New York. It might be noted that rainfall in Seattle is highest in the month of November, which is when the rates were being compared. At that time of year, New York was still enjoying the fall season, before the December and January cold fronts set in.

In 2020, along with the world, the United States suffered from the coronavirus pandemic, which cast a dark cloud over the country and affected the mood of many of its inhabitants. In 2018, before the pandemic, the *Seattle Times* reported that, between 2014 and 2016, Washington state's overall suicide rate increased 19 percent compared to the period between 1999 and 2001. Notably, the suicide rate in Puget Sound counties, outside of the Seattle metropolitan area, rose 29 percent, while the suicide rate in Seattle only rose 15 percent.. Thus, rates in Seattle were the lowest in the state of Washington, despite being higher than many other cities in the United States.[2]

To explain these disparities, we need to look at factors other than weather to explain the risk of suicide. We know, for example, that Montana, Alaska, and Wyoming have higher rates of suicide than the state of Washington does. We also know that rural areas have higher rates of suicide than metropolitan areas. That's because rural areas have less access to health care, and higher rates of social isolation, alcoholism, drug abuse, and gun ownership. We also know that gun ownership is correlated with high suicide rates due to its lethality. Interestingly, Seattle, an urban city with the lowest rate of suicide in the state of Washington, also has a relatively low rate of gun ownership. Seattle was also the first U.S. city to mandate that health-care workers complete training in risk assessment, management, and treatment of potentially suicidal individuals.[3]

Suicide is no more likely to occur in Seattle, than in any other area of the country, especially in areas with high rates of gun ownership, alcoholism, drug addiction, or poor access to healthcare—despite Seattle being portrayed as particularly suicide prone. In fact, the occurrence of suicide in Seattle is actually lower than in many areas that have high rates of gun ownership, addiction and poor healthcare.

While the weather may be a contributing factor to depression—and, therefore, suicide— there is no cause-and-effect relationship between a certain kind of weather and the number of suicides in that locale. This factor is important when trying to understand the meaning of suicide statistics. Essentially, no one factor by itself puts a person at risk. One must look at the whole picture.

APPENDIX 2
Statistical Overview of Suicide Rates Worldwide and in the United States

While not exhaustive, the following statistical overview reviews some of the categories that I found particularly interesting as I researched the topic of suicide. The material for each category proved enough to fill an entire book, so I am simply touching on the highlights.

Suicide around the Globe

Worldwide, the number of suicides has increased a staggering 60 percent in the last forty-five years.[1] Although rates of suicide in the United States are high, we are not even among the top ten countries. In 2019, the World Health Organization listed Lesotho as the top-ranking country for suicides, followed by Guyana, Eswatini, Kirbati, and Micronesia.[2] The statistics reflect the percentage per 100,000 people, rather than raw numbers. The rankings change all of the time, depending upon the organization, and the year. The Global Economy, for instance, cited Lithuania, Russia, Ukraine, Belarus, and Montenegro as the five top countries in 2019.[3] And, according to the World Population Review released in 2023, the top-ranking countries for suicides in 2019 were Lesotho, Guyana, Eswatini, South Korea, and Kiribati, with Micronesia further down the list.[4]

I was surprised to learn that some of the most troubled countries in the world showed lower rates of suicide, among them Syria, Iraq, and Afghanistan.[5] This makes sense, though, because many more people in that part of the world have died in battle, or from other medical causes, which serves to reduce the relative percentages of deaths by suicide.

Except for Belgium, Europe also shows a relatively low number of suicides. This includes formerly high-ranked Sweden. In fact, Norway, Sweden, Denmark, and Finland all have what researchers call very high "happiness rates."[6] It must be noted, however, that "happiness" is a relative term, and may vary from individual to individual, and from country to country.

My research also showed that some factors may offset the otherwise high rates of suicide one would expect. Religious and cultural attitudes, for example, may have a mediating effect, and serve to lower the rate of suicide in certain areas of the country—and even of the world—where faith in something of a higher power, and strong injunctions against suicide, prevail. Similarly, countries where day-to-day survival preoccupies one's attention, deaths by illness and war may preempt deaths by suicide. People in these countries may be focused on merely staying alive. A sense of community and belonging, in this case, may also be a mediating factor; where familial and community ties are strong, we can expect lower suicide rates.

Appendix 2

Suicide by Gender

As mentioned earlier, more men die of suicide than do women, regardless of race or country. The suicide rate for men is estimated to be as much as ten times higher than for women, depending on the country, or part of the world.[7] According to one report, the rates across Eastern Europe were six to seven times higher for men. In most countries, that number ranges from two to four times higher. But nearly 40 percent of countries in the world have more than fifteen suicide deaths per 100,000 men. Only 1.5 percent of countries showed a rate that high for women.[8]

The relative percentages also change by year. According to a 2020 study by the CDC (NCHS Date Brief No. 362, April 2020) authored by Holly Hedegaard, M.D, Sally C. Curtin, M.A. and Margaret Warner, PhD, suicide rates between 1999 and 2018 increased 35 percent. Rates for males were 3.5 to 4.5 times that number for females over the entire period. In 2018, the suicide rate for males was 3.7 times the rate for females.[9]

Men also demonstrate higher levels of "suicidal intent." That means, that when men decide to kill themselves, they are more intent on being successful. One study, for example, revealed that among older men, the intent to do "deliberate self-harm" was an important variable.[10]

Among women who kill themselves, the statistics are likewise variable regarding age. The age group with the highest number of female suicides appears to be among women between the ages of forty-five and sixty-four.[11] What struck me about this statistic, is that forty-five to sixty-four is the age when many women begin to deal with "empty-nest syndrome," and the effects of aging. One can speculate about whether during this particular age range, women feel that their purpose in life has been served, and that they have less reason to live than when they were young and life was full of possibility.

Interestingly, women are more often diagnosed with depression than men. On the other hand, women are more likely to seek help, and thus receive a diagnosis and treatment. It may be that if men sought help for their depressive symptoms and/or used less lethal means, they, too, would have lower suicide rates. Given that men are more intent on killing themselves, and tend to choose the most lethal means, they are not only more at risk, but are the most in need of early intervention. Unfortunately, mental-health professionals frequently observe that men in general are more reluctant to seek help from a primary physician for a physical illness—not to mention for a mental illness—because doing so demonstrates weakness. Instead, men prefer to self-medicate for as long as possible, which only increases depression, including that brought on by a physical ailment.

Helene Schumacher, in a 2019 BBC article, reported that the rate of male suicide was its lowest since 1981—5.5 deaths per 100,000. Suicide was still the single biggest killer of men under the age of forty-five in the United Kingdom. The U.K. rate for women, at the same time, was one third the rate for men.[12]

According to Schumacher, "Many societies have encouraged men to be 'strong' and not admit they're struggling. The result is that men are less likely to talk about their problems, not only to mental health specialists, but to friends and family." Quoting Colman O'Driscoll, former executive director of an Australian suicide prevention service, Schumacher adds that, "We condition boys from a very young age not to express emotion, because to express emotion is to be 'weak.'"[13] This is

Appendix 2

borne out by healthcare professionals who observe lower levels of crying or complaining by men.

Despite these tendencies, it is hard to say that men are, by nature, more suicidal. It might be safer to conclude that men and women manage their suicidal feelings differently. Their reasons for killing themselves also differ. It is interesting to note that, overall, the lowest rates for suicide are among Asian women.

While "gender-minority" status has been less studied than other groups until recently, a 2018 study identified differences among sexual minorities in terms of suicide. Their findings indicate that "heterosexist victimization, shame, and rejection sensitivity" were significant risk factors for suicide among this group.[14] More research is needed in this area.

Suicide by Age

Although the media, in recent years, has focused on suicide among young people, the highest rate for suicide is still among men seventy-five and older.[15] One possible explanation is that, unlike women, men—especially older men—tend to have fewer support systems, and are less inclined to reach out to others. This is particularly true after the death of a spouse. When men lose their wives later in life, they often become increasingly isolated, and suffer more from loneliness than do women, who are inclined to turn to other women for support.

Nevertheless, young people—adolescents and young adults— comprise the fastest growing group to harbor serious thoughts about suicide. According to the National Survey on Drug Use and Health (NSDUH), "Young adults aged eighteen to twenty-five in 2015 were more likely than adults in other age groups to have serious thoughts of suicide, to have made suicide plans, or to have attempted suicide.[16] It is noteworthy that the brain is not fully developed until about age twenty-six, and thus young adults in this age group are more immature in their judgments, and more impulsive in their behavior.

A disturbing statistic indicates that young women and girls might be becoming particularly at risk. Research shows that the gap between male and female suicide has been narrowing over the past few decades, especially among girls between ten and fourteen years old—a group that might not even have considered suicide a couple of decades ago.[17] A common explanation for this suicide trend is the proliferation of social media, and the increased bullying of young girls.

Reports by both the Center for Disease Control (CDC) and the National Institutes of Health (NIH) also show a doubling in suicide rates among females between 2007 and 2015. A recent CDC study revealed that one in three high-school-aged girls seriously considered suicide in 2021. The rate of "persistent sadness" among that group was double the rate for boys.[18]

Several studies report a growing trend of young girls using more violent means to kill themselves, including hanging and suffocation. Also of concern, is that women in general now more frequently use firearms as a means to kill themselves.[19] From 1960 to 1983, the rates of suicide by firearms and alcohol-related deaths increased among ten-to-nineteen-year-olds, and a report in June 2022, published by *Every Town*, claimed that "youth firearm suicide has reached its highest rate in more than 20 years."[20]

Appendix 2

An alarming number of drug-related deaths among young people was reported by the University of Washington, which said that "among people under 30, fentanyl-involved deaths started climbing statewide in 2016. By 2019 it had surpassed other opioid categories of deaths among that population, at the rate of four per 100,000. By 2020, fentanyl-involved deaths had doubled to eight per 100,000 among people under 30."[21] Not all of these deaths were directly related to suicide, but many could be considered involuntary suicides or what some call "accidental suicides."

In short, the numbers indicate an alarming increase in the rate of suicide among the youngest in our midst. Access to substances, legal and illegal, has had a dramatic effect on the rise in numbers. In addition, bullying, social media, racial hatred, and trauma are implicated as contributing factors to suicidal thoughts, and actions, by young people.

Suicide by Race and Ethnicity

Suicide among minorities appears more subject to political and socioeconomic factors, than among members of the majority culture in all countries—especially in the United States, which is among the most racially diverse countries in the world.

In terms of ethnicity in the States, which was my focus, suicide rates are highest among Native Americans, both male and female. However, suicidal ideation (thinking about killing oneself) varies by age and sex. The ideation rates are similar for Hispanics and whites (about 5 percent each), followed by blacks (4 percent) and Asians (3.6 percent). The highest rates are among American Indian and Alaskan youth, as well as those who are multi-racial.

Asian women have some of the lowest rates of suicide. The highest rates for women are among American Indians (10.5) and whites (8.3). With increasing racial attacks on Asians since the pandemic, we can expect the rates to rise in the Asian population. Surprisingly, young people of mixed race are even more vulnerable than single-race individuals, according to some studies. Statistics show that minorities, in general, are more at risk for suicide than whites, but in 2019, some studies revealed an ever-higher rate of attempts among mixed-race individuals.[22]

We can only speculate about the reasons for this trend. It might be that mixed-race youths have more difficulty fitting in and forming an identity, feeling that they are in a no-man's land, neither this nor that. My personal experience suggests that family dynamics in mixed-race families can also play a role, because the feelings between the two races within a given family may be divisive, especially among extended family members if they harbor negative feelings about the other race, or the cultural values of that side of the family. On the other hand, some mixed-race individuals (former U.S. President Barack Obama, for example) may manage to more easily cross racial lines and gain acceptance.

For men of every race, the number of suicides hovers around 12 percent, with Native American and white men having the highest rates. The lowest rates of suicide in 2019 were among black and Hispanic women and Asian and Pacific Islander women.[23]

As stress on minority populations grew during the coronavirus pandemic, so did the suicide rates. A study directed

Appendix 2

by Paul Nestadt, which analyzed suicides among residents of Maryland, found a 45 percent decrease in suicides among white residents during the early part of 2020, while the rate for black residents increased 94 percent. Nestadt, co-director of the Johns Hopkins Anxiety Clinic, noted, "This is obviously concerning, and it serves as a reminder that when we aggregate all our data—thinking the population is homogeneous—we miss especially vulnerable populations." He speculated that white residents might have had "greater supports" during the first pandemic peak or had "a deeper economic cushion to ride out the shutdown."[24] The trend was also noted in the New York Times, and other publications, including Healthday, which reported a doubling of suicides among black people during the 2019 coronavirus disease (COVID-19) lockdowns.[25] At the same time, suicides among whites were cut in half.

This data points to the importance of the political climate of a society, and of how groups within that society are treated—or mistreated. In homogeneous societies, the chances for equal treatment are higher than in nations with a great deal of diversity. Diversity tends to split society into superior and inferior groups, with certain subgroups treated as if they are of lesser value.

When human rights are honored, there is less reason to end one's life. Instead, people enjoy a sense of belonging and purpose. As we have seen, during times when people are forced by circumstances—such as war, national, and international crises, and national disasters—to come together, suicide rates go down. This suggests that the social, political, psychological, and spiritual values in which a person's life is embedded all impact their life and death choices, whether consciously or not.

Suicide by Occupation

We all know that work can be stressful, but it appears from the data that workers in some occupations are more vulnerable to stress than others, and may thus have higher rates of suicide. According to a CDC report, in 2017 nearly 38,000 people of working age (sixteen to sixty-four years) in the United States died by suicide, which represented a 40 percent increase in less than two decades.[26]

Studies also show that suicide rates are significantly higher in five major industry groups: 1) mining, quarrying, and oil-and-gas extraction; 2) construction; 3) other service-oriented industries e.g., automotive repair; 4) agriculture, forestry, fishing, and hunting; and 5) transportation and warehousing—most of which are male-dominated industries.[27]

In addition, higher rates of suicide are found among certain occupational groups. These include: 1) construction and extraction; 2) installation, maintenance, and repair; 3) arts, design, entertainment, sports, and media; 4) transportation and material moving; 5) protective service; and 6) healthcare support. Although no explanations are offered for the higher rates of suicide within these particular occupations, ironically, many of these jobs attract their share of females.[28]

The profession of physicians, including veterinarians, also has a surprisingly high rate of suicide. According to one study, the suicide risk among doctors is five to seven times higher than that in the general population.[29] Another study estimated that rate to be as much as 40 percent higher.[30] According to a report by the American College of Emergency Physicians, "Each year in the U.S., roughly 300 to 400 physicians die by

Appendix 2

suicide."[31] In fact, another study estimated that 4 percent of all physician deaths are by suicide, and that an estimated 9 percent of physicians are said to report suicidal thoughts.[32]

Most studies attribute the high rates of physician suicide to the inherent stress of the job, and the possibility that doctors are less inclined to seek treatment for depression or other mental disorders, fearing that their practice may suffer if word of their own need for professional help is revealed. Other stresses cited by various studies include burnout, loneliness, and high divorce rates.

It is common knowledge that doctors suffer from long hours, demanding patients, malpractice lawsuits, the pressure to pay for medical-school expenses and continued education, and an ease of access to medications. This last factor may distinguish the practice of medicine from other professions. It is understood that the ease with which depressed doctors can obtain medication contributes to the increase in suicides within this group. A doctor is also extremely knowledgeable regarding doses of medications and combinations that will be fatal if inhaled, injected, or swallowed. In fact, evidence shows that doctors are nearly four times as likely to use drugs as a suicide method, in contrast the otherwise most lethal means: firearms.[33]

Further, medical students are not exempt from these statistics, either. Estimates are that 9.4 percent of fourth-year medical students and residents suffer from suicidal thoughts, according to the AMA Medical Student Association, which reports that medical students are three times more likely to commit suicide than their same-age peers.[34] Studies also show that compassion among medical students diminishes during the four years of medical school.[35]

The number of medical students I interviewed while researching this book cited long hours, less credit for accomplishments and more blame for mistakes, as well as less power of decision making as sources of stress. At the same time, one study reveals the positive effect of empathy toward medical students during their training.[36] It seems that empathy begets empathy.

Each year the National Institute for Occupational Safety & Health (NIOSH) compiles a list of the jobs with the highest suicide rates. An article in Mental Health Daily is quoted as saying, "It seems as though in the United States, jobs requiring significant levels of aptitude, sacrifice, and education seem to be those with above-average risk of suicide."[37]

One article listed the jobs with the highest suicide risk as those being doctors, dentists, police officers, veterinarians, financial-services workers, real-estate agents, electricians, lawyers, farmers, and pharmacists (in that order).[38] In contrast to the male-dominated professions, these occupations employ their share of both men and women.

In 2018, television news network CNN reported high suicide rates among women in the following fields:

- Arts, design, entertainment, sports, and media—jobs such as illustrator, animator, tattooist, and professional sports player
- Protective service—jobs such as police officer, private investigator, and transportation security-administration worker
- Health care support—jobs such as dental assistant, massage therapist, and pharmacy aide[39]

Appendix 2

    I find it interesting that other high-stress jobs, such as air traffic controllers, and professions that employ crisis workers, were not listed. However, we know that police officers, firefighters, and soldiers experience extreme stress. In his State of the Union Address on February 7, 2023, U.S. President Joe Biden noted that each day, seventeen veterans die by suicide.

    For both men and women, the fields with the lowest suicides rates are education, training, and library science, which includes teachers, professors, and archivists.[40] With the threat of school shootings, however, the stress on teachers and other school-based professions has increased, which may in turn, increase the rates of suicide among this population. On the other hand, this group is more likely to seek treatment for their stress, in part because women comprise most of this field.

Socioeconomic Factors

As indicated above, socioeconomic factors play an important role in determining the up-and-down rates of suicide. During times of economic downturn, when unemployment rates increase, so do suicide rates, typically eighteen to twenty-four months following an economic decline. According to a recent study reported by Lisa Firestone, among twenty-six European Union countries, for every 1 percent increase in unemployment there was a .79 percent increase in suicides among people under the age of sixty-five.[41] Firestone also reports on a U.S. study by economist, Christopher J. Ruhm, which shows that each increase in a state's unemployment rate of 1 percent raises the number of suicides in the state by 1.3 percent.[42]

Since a person's health insurance is often linked to their employment, access to mental-health services may be unavailable when a person is unemployed. Isolation is also a factor during times of unemployment, and we know that isolation is linked to an increase in suicides. The opposite is true during more lucrative times. According to an article published by the Wiley online library, there is an inverse relation between stock-market returns and the percentage of increase in suicide rates.[43]

All of this data furthers supports the idea that when a society cares for the least wealthy of its citizens, everyone benefits. In a study, which shows an overall decrease in suicide rates between 1970 and 2002, the authors speculate that an increase in healthy life expectancy may have contributed to the decrease in suicides during this time. The study's authors speculated that "as individuals live longer, maintaining both close relationships and relatively better health, feelings of loneliness and depression and being a burden to the family are delayed, and the risk for suicide may be reduced." They point out, however, that this positive likelihood is higher among the oldest age groups, who are more inclined to feel lonely, depressed, and burdensome to begin with.[44]

Suicide versus Homicide

Comparisons between the highest rates for suicide versus homicide vary from year to year. A startling statistic in 2018, revealed that more people died from suicide than from homicide, although the rate of homicides, including mass shootings, had been climbing since 2015.[45] The National Institute of Mental

Appendix 2

Health cited a study by the Centers for Disease Control and Prevention (CDC) WISQARS in its "Leading Causes of Death Reports" that in 2020, there were nearly two times as many suicides (45,979) in the United States as there were homicides (24,576).[46] In other years, more homicides than suicides were reported, which has led researchers to wonder whether there truly is a link between the two causes of death.

While suicide was the twelfth leading cause of death overall in 2020, it was the second leading cause among individuals between the ages of ten and fourteen and twenty-five and thirty-four.[47] However, suicides dropped during the COVID-19 pandemic when the country was under lock down. These numbers were obscured by increasing numbers of suicides among alcohol and drug users, teens, and minorities. During the pandemic, a study in Maryland showed that suicides among white residents decreased by 45 percent between early March and early May, while suicides among black residents increased by 94 percent during those same months. Johns Hopkins published the results.[48]

Karen Blum, cited a *U.S. News and World Report* article, which reported that suicide among blacks doubled during the pandemic, and it blamed income disparities, and lack of health care, as contributing factors. Dr. Paul Sasha Nestadt, assistant professor of psychiatry at the Johns Hopkins School of Medicine in Baltimore, and author of a study on the economic impact of COVID-19, stated that "when someone is struck hard by things around the pandemic and they can't get access to good mental-health care, they are in the most danger."[49] He was speaking in particular of the economic effects on black people. As we have seen, factors such as economics, and access to healthcare, affect rates of suicide.

The statistics on suicide during COVID-19 did not take into account those who considered suicide, but did not act on it. One report by the CDC, however, found that approximately twice as many respondents in June of 2020 reported seriously considering suicide compared with those in 2018. In fact, phone calls to the national mental-health crisis hotline in March of 2020 was 891 percent higher than the year before.[50]

As noted earlier, during the early phase of a natural disaster, there's a sense of community building, a feeling that we're all in this together. That may have been the case in the early stages of COVID-19. However, the income disparities and racial tensions that increased during the pandemic gave rise to unprecedented polarization in the country, which deflated any sense of togetherness. Since the pandemic, U.S. polarization has only increased, leading to more alienation and hostility. Chances are, both homicide and suicide rates may rise in such a sociopolitical climate.

Suicide and Violence

Some researchers have suggested a link between suicide and violence, which is not surprising given that individuals who have experienced violence are more likely to become violent themselves. The violence may be directed toward oneself, or toward others, or both. An article in the University of Washington News (*UW News*) seems to suggest that more often, violence is directed toward oneself. The authors state that "in the United States, suicide is twice as common as homicide—and more often involves firearms." The article is based on a study by the

Appendix 2

University of Washington, Northeastern University, and Harvard University. The study's lead author, Erin Morgan, hopes that the findings may impact gun ownership. *UW News* quotes her as saying, "Knowing that the presence of a firearm increases the risk for suicide, and that firearm suicide is substantially more common than firearm homicide, may lead people to think twice about whether or not firearm ownership and their storage practices are really the safest option for them and their household."[51]

This not to say that people who commit suicide are inherently more violent. An estimated 30 percent of violent individuals have a history of self-destructive behavior, while only 10 to 20 percent of suicidal persons have a history of violent behavior.[52]

The distinguishing factor may be the degree of open expression of hostility and rage that is available to the angry individual. We saw an example of this earlier in the story of my brother, who was unable to express anger in constructive ways, and ended up turning that anger onto other people and, eventually, himself. The same was true of my client, Charlie, whom I discussed earlier in the book. On the other hand, I have experienced clients verbalize in disturbing detail the kind of violence that they might wish upon another person, or society in general, but their ability to verbally express their violent thoughts in therapy sessions, and to work through their angry feelings, diminished their need to act upon those feelings.

The link between violence and suicide may be more valid among young people who have not yet learned healthy ways of coping with anger, or are more impulsive. Psychological autopsies of young suicide victims indicate higher levels of aggression than among older age groups. Such statistics may indicate that young people, especially males with aggressive and antisocial behavior, are more likely to commit suicide than are young men who are simply depressed, and that as people age, aggression and impulsivity play a lesser role. As the authors of one article say, "Nonviolent suicide methods, potential markers of lower levels of lifetime aggression, are associated with older suicides."[53] This has certainly been my experience in working with men of all ages. Based on my experience, and the research I've accumulated over the years, it seems that anger, even more than depression, needs to be addressed by mental health professionals.

There may also be a link between violence and suicide within gender-minority populations. Findings from a 2021 survey showed high levels of violence, depression, and suicidal thoughts among lesbian, gay, and bisexual youth. According to the *New York Times*, "More than one in five of these students reported attempting suicide in the year before."[54]

Suicidal Ideation

Suicide rates are further complicated by the number of people who attempt suicide without success, and others who merely consider it. This is true in all segments of society. In 2019, for example, an estimated 12 million Americans thought seriously about committing suicide, 3.5 million planned a suicide attempt, and 1.4 million carried out a failed attempt.[55] These figures do not include people who seemingly died of other causes, commonly referred to in psychological circles as "covert suicides." These are deaths that are subsumed under such categories as suspicious

Appendix 2

car, or other types, of "accidents." This group could include people who provoke police officers to kill them (to which the familiar term "Death by Cop" could apply) as well as people who slowly die of alcoholism, or chronically engage in high-risk behaviors. Some of these individuals may not mean to kill themselves, at least not consciously, but they are in a constant dance with death.

Common Means for Ending One's Life

Although use of firearms is the most common lethal means of killing oneself, it is not the only one. Jumping off of a bridge or building, while less common, is equally lethal, meaning the attempt almost always results in a successful suicide. It must be emphasized, however, that overall, twice as many people die from firearms (54 percent) than from the next most common means.[56] Because more men than women own and use firearms, it makes sense that more men are successful in their attempt.

It is estimated that six in ten persons who own a gun in the United States are men, and firearms account for over 50 percent of suicides. In 2017, about 56 percent of men died by gunshot wounds, compared with 31.2 percent of women.[57] Women generally tend to use less lethal means, such as overdosing, according to most studies.

We can only wonder what the rates of suicide would be without the proliferation of guns in the United States. Thirty-seven percent of American households owned one or more guns in 2020. Gun ownership has risen and fallen over the last few decades, with a high of 47 percent in 1990 and a low of

37 percent in 2014. However, as we have seen, the numbers have risen since the coronavirus disease pandemic. In 2022, gun ownership in the United States was 45 percent, according to Statista.[58]

The numbers for gun ownership rose higher for men than for women, and higher for white men than for any other ethnic group.[59] Gun ownership has also been shown to be higher among Republicans than Democrats, according to a study by the Pew Research group.[60] Metropolitan areas also have higher rates, as do states in the South. The Northeast has the lowest percentage of gun ownership. In addition, most gun owners are white, and live in rural areas, especially in the western part of the country, although suicide by firearms is highest in the South.

While owning a gun does not predispose a person to suicide, one can make the case that having access to a gun increases the likelihood of a successful suicide attempt if one is suicidal.

Because statistics on suicide and its contributing factors were not compiled in any systematic way until recently, we have no way of knowing what the numbers were in earlier times. The first recorded suicide was made around 2000 B.C, but it was not until Emile Durkheim's empirical studies in 1897 that data was formally collected, although rough estimates were made as early as the Middle Ages, and the Greeks recognized suicide, even if they had no formal data. Clearly, suicide is not something new to humankind, and certainly not limited to the United States, although much of my focus has been on suicide in the United States.

APPENDIX 3
Neurobiological and Genetic Factors in Suicide

Biology, neuroscience, and neurobiology, as well as genetics, have added to the store of knowledge about suicide in recent years. Editor, Yogesh Dwivedi's, *The Neurobiological Basis of Suicide* is one of the most comprehensive books on the brain and suicide. In it, he compiles essays by leading experts on the relationship between neurobiology, psychology, and social–emotional factors associated with suicidality. One of those experts is Jan Fawcett, who points out that suicide occurs across diagnoses, primarily including clinical depression, bipolar disorder, severe anxiety, and increased impulsivity, the cause of which is multivariate.[1]

The book cites numerous studies by various researchers on the effect of chronic risk factors such as early childhood abuse, stress, and substance abuse, as well as living alone, a history of past or recent attempts, and severe impulse problems. In addition, acute risk factors such as severe anxiety, insomnia, a sudden increase in impulsivity or worsening of clinical symptoms, hopelessness, and certain situational factors, are often of a psychological or spiritual nature. Interestingly, 30 to 70 percent of suicides occur in patients already receiving treatment, while

95 percent of people who have some form of a psychiatric illness do not commit suicide, suggesting that suicide is not predictable in the individual, but results rather, from a complex series of factors.[2]

Many of the studies included in Dwivedi's book focus on hospitalized patients, and much of the research on brain abnormalities has been done postmortem. Research suggests deficits in noradrenergic signaling, serotonergic neurotransmission, and altered neuroplasticity are factors, as well as several other brain-system problems related to depression, impulsivity, and anxiety. Environmental conditions can also lead to alterations in brain neurochemistry that can increase the risk of suicide. In the preface, Dwivedi himself talks about epigenetic changes, which are modifications in the DNA that regulate whether genes are turned on or off. As he states, "Until recently it was believed that only physical and chemical environmental factors altered epigenetic marking; more recently, lawsuits have indicated that the social environment can also induce epigenetic changes."[3] The factor of early-life adversity aligns with the above statistics on impoverished populations. Genetic factors also play a role, suggesting that our environment can change our DNA.

While characteristics in young people have been less studied, what researchers have found is that, in general, impulsivity is more of a problem in adolescents and is considered a major factor in suicidality among this age group, while cognitive decline and impaired decision-making may make the elderly more at risk.[4]

In *Why People Die of Suicide*, Thomas Joiner cites studies implicating several genetic and neurobiological factors contributing to suicide. For example, identical twins are more likely to commit suicide than fraternal twins. There is also a higher incidence of suicide in adopted children whose biological parents suicided.[5] From his research, he concluded that "a family history of suicide appears to contribute about a twofold increase in risk." That number increases or decreases based on how many family members committed suicide, as well as on how closely they were related.[6]

In keeping with other researchers, Joiner points to the serotonin-transporter gene. Serotonin is a chemical that plays a key role in mood, sleep, sexual desire, and other bodily functions. Says Joiner, "There is some emerging consensus that those with the s/s genotype have more dysregulated serotonin systems and thus are more prone to attendant problems."[7] A genotype is a unique sequence of DNA. He found, for example, that people with significant family histories of suicide were more likely to have the s/s genotype than were those without a family history. Joiner himself has this genotype, and has a family history of suicide.

Like Dwivedi, Joiner seems to suggest that there is a genetic component to suicidal behavior, and that the genetic risk appears to be at least partly independent of the risk for mental illness, which means that one may not have a mental illness, but rather a genetic predisposition to suicide. He also agrees with Dwivedi about the role of impulsivity in suicide, believing it is indirectly associated with suicidal behavior. Joiner explains it this way: "Disruptions in serotonin-system functioning may predispose people to an array of impulsive behaviors, which may, in turn, reduce fear of provocative experiences. These experiences may lead to the acquired ability to enact lethal self-injury and thus to increased risk for completed suicide."[8]

Whether this genetic component was at play in my own family is uncertain. However, other factors were handed down that are not genetic, including shame, and fear of poverty, as well as an injunction against expressing feelings. Anyone suffering from all these factors, in addition to a genetic predisposition to suicide, would certainly be at risk. However, there is always the possibility of mitigating factors, which include at least one positive and supportive relationship with another person, a spiritual or otherwise meaningful life experience, and an inherent resiliency.

NOTES

For full citations, see the bibliography.

Introduction

1. United Nations, "800,000 People Commit Suicide Each Year."
2. Kaieteur News, "Suicide Rates Increased by 60 Percent Worldwide."
3. Dastagir, "More and More Americans Are Dying by Suicide."
4. Joiner, *Why People Die by Suicide*, 4–7.
5. Martin, "Anthony Bourdain's Death."
6. Ibid.
7. Ibid.
8. Holloway, "Whale of Pain."

Chapter 1

Epigraph: Hillman, *Suicide and the Soul*.
1. Jung, *Aion*, 70–71.

Chapter 2

Epigraph: Mueller et al., "Social Roots of Suicide."
1. Hedegaard et al., "Increase in Suicide Mortality."

2. Dastagir, "More and More Americans Are Dying by Suicide."
3. Yoon, "Suicide in South Korea."
4. Hedegaard et al., "Increase in Suicide Mortality."

Chapter 3

Epigraph: Pridmore et al., "Two Mistaken Beliefs."
1. Asomatou et al., "The Act of Suicide in Greek Mythology."
2. Ibid.
3. Missouri University School of Medicine, "What Is Euthanasia?"
4. Bible Tools, "Strong's #849: Autocheir."
5. Etymology Online Dictionary, "Euthanize."
6. Oxford Reference, "Euthanasia."
7. Wikipedia, "Senicide."
8. Ibid.
9. Ibid.
10. Magnier, "In Southern India."
11. Mathew, "Thalaikoothal."
12. Magnier, "In Southern India."
13. Best, "Suicide: An Archetypal Perspective."
14. Maiese et al., "A Peculiar Case of Suicide."
15. Wikipedia, "Suicide in Antiquity."
16. Asomatou et al., "The Act of Suicide in Greek Mythology."
17. Ibid.
18. Cholbi, "Suicide."
19. Ibid.
20. Wikipedia, "Suicide in Antiquity."
21. Cholbi, "Suicide."
22. Wikipedia, "Philosophy of Suicide."
23. Ibid.

Notes

24. Seneca. "On the Proper Time to Slip the Cable."
25. Cicero, *De Officiis*, 3:60–61.
26. Camus, *Myth of Sisyphus*, 3.
27. Middleton, "The 'Noble Death' of Judas Iscariot."
28. Ibid.
29. Cherry, "Freud's Theories of Life and Death Instincts."
30. Roarty, "Death Wishing and Cultural Memory: A Walk Through Japan's Suicide Forest." Brill. P 89-100.
31. Kristy Puchko, "15 Eerie Things about Japan's Suicide Forest."

Chapter 4

Epigraph: Jung, *Structure and Dynamics of the Psyche*, para. 577.
1. Lorenz, "Ancient Theories of Soul."
2. Ibid.
3. Wisdom Library, "Ātmāhuti,"
4. Brittanica, "Anatta."
5. Hillman, *Suicide and the Soul*, 11.
6. Ibid., 36.
7. Ibid., 39.
8. Ibid., 39.
9. Ibid., 43.

Chapter 5

Epigraph: Jung, *C. G. Jung Letters, Vol. 2*, 25.
1. Jung, *C. G. Jung Letters, Vol. 1*, 279.
2. Jung, *C. G. Jung Letters, Vol. 2*, 25.
3. Ibid., 434.
4. Ibid., 435–436.

5. Ibid.
6. Jung, *Psychological Types*, para. 573.
7. Jung. *Two Essays*, para. 192.
8. Ibid.
9. Jung. *Structure and Dynamics of the Psyche*, para. 547.
10. Jung, *Practice of Psychotherapy*, para. 128.
11. Purrington, "Carl Jung's Views on Suicide—Quotations."
12. Gersch, "Suicide and the Soul."

Chapter 6

Epigraph: Jung, *C. G. Jung Letters, Vol. 1*, 435–36.
1. Cherry, "Freud's Eros and Thanatos Theory."
2. Goethe, quoted by Szasz, "Suicide as a Moral Issue."
3. Bradvik, "Suicide Risk and Mental Disorders."
4. Harkavy-Friedman, "Ask Dr. Jill."
5. Ibid.
6. Pompili et al., "Suicide Risk in Depression and Bipolar Disorder."
7. Harkavy-Friedman, "Ask Dr. Jill."
8. Bradvik, "Suicide Risk," 1–2.
9. Harkavy-Friedman, "Ask Dr. Jill."
10. Szasz, "Suicide as a Moral Issue."
11. Gersch, "Suicide and The Soul."
12. Ibid.
13. Ibid.
14. Joiner, *Why People Die by Suicide*, 103.
15. The Counselling Directory, "Psychodynamics of Suicide."
16. Ahlzen, "Suffering, Authenticity, and Physician Assisted Suicide."
17. Best, "Suicide: An Archetypal Perspective," 73.

18. Hendin, "Psychodynamics of Suicide."
19. Klopfer, "Suicide: The Jungian Point of View," 196–97.
20. All biblical quotes in the book are from the New King James Version.
21. Joiner, *Why People Die by Suicide*, 38.
22. Shneidman, *The Suicidal Mind*.
23. Joiner, ibid.
24. Ibid., 136.
25. Ibid., 134.
26. Ibid., 121.
27. Ibid., 22.
28. Shneidman, *The Suicidal Mind*, 4.
29. Ibid., 7–8.
30. Ibid., 8.
31. Ibid., 7.
32. Ibid., 13.

Chapter 7

Epigraph: Brown, quoted in Cook, "What Is Shame and How Does It Show Up in Your Life and Work?"
1. Jacoby, *Shame and the Origins of Self-Esteem*, x.
2. Willie, "The Shame of Existing."
3. Ibid.
4. DeYoung, *Understanding and Treating Chronic Shame*, preface.
5. Inman et al., "Human Amygdala Stimulation Effects."
6. Piretti et al., "The Role of Amygdala in Self-Conscious Emotions."
7. Pulcu et al., "Increased Amygdala Response to Shame."
8. Ibid.

9. Kalafat and Lester, "Shame and Suicide."
10. Ibid.
11. Tomkins Institute, "Nine Affects."
12. Ibid.
13. Lester, "Role of Shame in Suicide."
14. Fishkin, *Science of Shame and Its Treatment*, 21.
15. Tangney.
16. Ibid. Abstract.
17. Kalafat and Lester, "Shame and Suicide"; see also Lewis, *Shame: The Exposed Self*.
18. Brown, *Atlas of the Heart;* see also Oprah's interviews of Brown on "Super Soul Sunday."
19. Hallowell, "ADHD and Shame."
20. Taylor-Jones, "When Shame Becomes Deadly."
21. Ibid.
22. Tanasugarn, "Spotting the Triggers in Covert Narcissism."
23. Mcleod, "Erik Erikson's Stages of Psychosocial Development."
24. Ibid.
25. Ibid.
26. Ibid
27. Ibid.
28. Best, "Suicide: An Archetypal Perspective"; Kaufman's quote is from *The Psychology of Shame*, 5–18.
29. Tomkins, SS. *Affect, Imagery and Consciousness*. Vol. 2, p.118. New York: Springer & Co., 1963.
30. Kaufman, Gershen. Journal of Counseling Psychology, 1974. Vol. 21, No 6, p.1.
31. Edelman, Sandra. *Turning the Gorgon: A Meditation on Shame*. Woodstock, CT: Spring Publications, 1998, 34.
32. Ibid., Best, quoting Edelman, *Turning the Gorgon*, 34.

33. Nietzsche, quoted in *Goodreads*.
34. American Journal of Play, "Playing on the Right Side of the Brain."
35. DeYoung, *Understanding and Treating Chronic Shame*, xiii.
36. Ibid., 7.
37. Ibid.
38. Jacoby, *Shame*, 22.
39. Jung, *Answer to Job*.
40. Edinger, *Ego and Archetype*, 82.
41. Ibid., 85.
42. Ibid., 91.
43. Edinger, *Encounter with the Self*, 11.
44. Edinger, *Ego and Archetype*, 91.
45. Ibid., 80.

Chapter 8

Epigraph: Andrew Edmund Slaby, "Creativity, Depression and Suicide."
1. McCall and Black, "Link between Suicide and Insomnia."
2. Psych Central. "Freud's Theory of Depression and Guilt."
3. Ibid.
4. Ibid.
5. Jung, *Symbols of Transformation*, para 625. Also see Sharp, *Primer of Jungian Concepts*.
6. Ibid.
7. Depression defined: see *DSM-5*, 94–97.
8. Ibid., 97–99.
9. Hollis, *Swamplands*, 68.
10. Goldblatt, "Psychodynamics of Hope in Suicidal Despair."
11. Hollis, *Swamplands*, 76.

12. Hendin, "Psychodynamics of Suicide."
13. Harding, *Value and Meaning of* Depression, 5.
14. Ibid., 5–6.
15. Ibid., 9.
16. Hollis, *Swamplands*, 77.
17. Ibid., 80.
18. Best, "Suicide: An Archetypal Perspective," 67.
19. Ibid., 80.
20. Ibid.
21. Ibid.
22. Rosen, *Transforming Depression*, 61.
23. Ibid., xxv.
24. Ibid., xxiii.
25. Ibid., xxiv.
26. Ibid., xxv.
27. Woodman, *Pregnant Virgin*, 14.
28. Estés, *Women Who Run with the Wolves*, 232–33.
29. Ibid., 72.

Chapter 9

Epigraph: Van der Kolk, *Body Keeps the* Score, 43.
1. American Psychiatric Association, "What Is Posttraumatic Stress Disorder (PTSD)?"
2. Unyte, "What Is Trauma?"
3. Contreras, "Unveiling the Brain's Role in Modern Trauma Treatment."
4. Crisis House, "What Is Trauma?"
5. Ashley Olivine, "What is Trauma?"
6. Miezio, "Know the 7 Types of Trauma Like a Psychotherapist."
7. Marschall, "The Four Fear Responses."

Notes

8. Joseph, "What is Trauma?"
9. Montgomery County Emergency Service, "Trauma and Suicide Risk."
10. Unyte, "What Is Trauma?"
11. Post-traumatic stress disorder defined: *DSM-5*, 143–49.
12. Thatcher, "Can Emotional Trauma Cause Brain Damage?"
13. Ibid.
14. S. K. Goldsmith et al., eds., *Reducing Suicide*.
15. Ibid, see subhead, "Childhood Sexual Abuse and Population Attributable Risk for Suicide."
16. Ibid., see subhead, "Modifying Factors."
17. Clements-Nolle et al., "Childhood Trauma and Risk for Past and Future Suicide Attempts."
18. Ibid.
19. Mind, "Post-Traumatic Stress Disorder," quoted in Leonard, "What is Trauma? What to Know."
20. Ibid., Mind.
21. Unyte, "What is Trauma?"
22. Pigeon et al., "Sleep Disturbance Preceding Suicide among Veterans."
23. Davis et al., "Post-Traumatic Stress Disorder and Suicidal Ideation."
24. Bonner interviewing Thorne in "Rurality's Relationship to Suicide Risk." See also Thorne et al., "Traumatic Stress and Suicide Risk."
25. Ibid., Bonner interviewing Thorne.
26. Tick, *War and the Soul*.

Chapter 10

Epigraph: Jung, *Man and His Symbols*.

1. Jung, *Practice of Psychotherapy*, para. 470.
2. Brehier, *History of Philosophy*, 208.
3. Edinger, *Ego and Archetype*, 10.
4. Ibid., 11.
5. Hollis. *Living Between Worlds*, 3.
6. Ibid.
7. Estés, *Women Who Run with the Wolves*, 395.
8. Ibid., 449.
9. Ibid., 450.

Chapter 11

Epigraph: Taylor-Jones, "When Shame Becomes Deadly."
1. Edinger, *Anatomy of the Psyche*, 85.
2. Ibid., 86.
3. Jung, *Mysterium Coniunctionis*, para. 151.
4. Edinger, *Anatomy of the Psyche*, 87.
5. Ibid., 88.
6. Ibid., 90.
7. Ibid., 90–91.
8. Jung, *Mysterium Coniunctionis*, para. 683.
9. Edinger, *Anatomy of the Psyche*, 91.
10. Ibid., 85.
11. Ibid., 5.

Chapter 12

Epigraph: Hollis, *The Goal of Life Is not Happiness but Meaning. Swamplands of the Soul; New Life in Dismal Places*, 8.
1. Allphin, "An Unhealable Wound."
2. Richards, "Cohabitation and the Negative Therapeutic Reaction."
3. Sinason, "Who Is the Mad Voice Inside?"

Notes

4. Young, "Across the Borderline."
5. Richards, "Cohabitation."
6. Auden, quoted in *Goodreads*.
7. Woodman, *Pregnant Virgin*, 40–41.
8. Mikhailova, "Suicide in Psychoanalysis."
9. Hendin, "Psychodynamics of Suicide," 159.
10. See Raphling, "Dreams and Suicide Attempts."
11. Hendin, "Psychodynamics of Suicide," 159.
12. Ibid., 160.
13. Ibid.
14. Taylor-Jones, "A Mother's Death, A Daughter's Birth."
15. Mikhailova, "Suicide in Psychoanalysis," 20.
16. Wheelwright, *The Death of a Woman*.
17. Sulaiman, "You Will Be Somebody's Ancestor. Act Accordingly."
18. Jung, *Structure and Dynamics of the Psyche*, para. 686.
19. Hollis, *Swamplands*, 11.

Appendix 1

1. Balk, "Seattle Was the Saddest Metro Area."
2. Balk, "Suicide Rate up in All Regions of Washington."
3. Ibid.

Appendix 2

1. Kaieteur News, "Suicide Rates Increased by 60 Percent Worldwide."
2. Wikipedia, "List of Countries by Suicide Rate" (WHO statistics).
3. Global Economy, "Suicides—Country Rankings."
4. World Population Review, "Suicide Rate by Country 2023."

5. Ibid.
6. World Population Review, "Best Countries to Live in 2023."
7. Saloni Dattani et al., "Suicides."
8. Ibid.
9. Hedegaard et al., "Increase in Suicide Mortality." -
10. Freeman et al, "A Cross-National Study on Gender Differences in Suicide Intent."
11. Hedegaard et al., "Increase in Suicide Mortality."
12. Schumacher, "Why More Men than Women Die by Suicide."
13. Ibid.
14. Mereish et al., "Minority Stress and Relational Mechanisms of Suicide among Sexual Minorities."
15. Hedegaard et al., "Increase in Suicide Mortality."
16. Piscopo et al., "Suicidal Thoughts and Behavior among Adults."
17. Chatterjee, "U.S. Suicide Rates Are Rising Faster among Women than Men."
18. Flanagan, "Teen Girls Report Record Levels of Sadness,"
19. Branigin, "More Women than Ever Own Guns."
20. Everytown, "The Rise of Firearm Suicide among Young Americans."
21. UW Medicine, "State Data Reveal Fentanyl's Fatal Role across Age Groups."
22. Troya et al., "Suicide Rates among Individuals from Ethic Minority Backgrounds."
23. Suicide Prevention Resource Center, "Scope of the Problem."
24. Blum, "Suicides Rise in Black Population."
25. Rabin, "U.S. Suicides Declined Overall in 2020"; see also Mann, "Pandemic Tied to Higher Suicide Rate in Blacks."
26. Peterson et al., "Suicide Rates by Industry and Occupation."
27. Ibid.

28. Ibid.
29. Ventriglio et al., "Suicide among Doctors: A Narrative Review."
30. Kalmoe et al., "Physician Suicide: A Call to Action."
31. Matheson, "Physician Suicide."
32. Advisory Board, "Charted: Physicians' Mental Health in 2023."
33. Samarasekera et al., "Development of Student Empathy during Medical Education."
34. Paturel, "Healing the Very Youngest Healers."
35. Batt-Rawden et al., "Teaching Empathy to Medical Students."
36. Samarasekera, "Development of Student Empathy."
37. Mental Health Daily, "Top 11 Professions with Highest Suicide Rates."
38. Choices Psychotherapy, "Top 10 Jobs with Highest Suicide Rates."
39. Thomas, "These Jobs Have Highest Suicide Rates."
40. Ibid.
41. Firestone, "The Anti-Self vs. the True Self."
42. Ibid.
43. Wisniewski et al., "Do Stock Market Fluctuations Affect Suicide Rates?"
44. McKeown et al., "US Suicide Rates by Age Group, 1970–2002."
45. Sheats et al., "Surveillance for Violent Deaths."
46. National Institute of Mental Health, "Suicide Is a Leading Cause of Death."
47. Ibid.
48. Blum, "Suicides Rise in Black Population."
49. Nestadt, quoted in University of Rochester Medical Center, "Pandemic Tied to Higher Suicide Rate."

50. Czeisler et al., "Mental Health, Substance Use, and Suicidal Ideation."
51. University of Washington, "Suicide More Prevalent than Homicide in US."
52. Plutchik and van Praag, "Psychosocial Correlates of Suicide and Violence Risk."
53. McGirr et al., "Impulsive-Aggressive Behaviors and Completed Suicide."
54. Ghorayshi and Rabin, "Teen Girls Report Record Levels of Sadness."
55. Stone et al., "Changes in Suicide Rates."
56. Gramlich, "What the Data Says about Gun Deaths."
57. Everytown, "Gun Violence in America."
58. Statista, "Gun ownership in the U.S. 1972–2022."
59. Parker et al., "The Demographics of Gun Ownership."
60. Ibid.

Appendix 3

1. Jan Fawcett, "Diagnosis, Traits, States, and Comorbidity in Suicide," in Dwivedi, ed., *Neurological Basis of Suicide.*
2. Dwivedi, *Neurobiological Basis of Suicide*, xv.
3. Ibid., xvii.
4. Ibid., xvii–xviii.
5. Joiner, *Why People Die by Suicide*, 175–76.
6. Ibid., 174.
7. Ibid., 177.
8. Ibid., 187.

BIBLIOGRAPHY

Abramson, Ashley. Quoting Jena Field in "The Science of Shame." *Elemental* (July 22, 2020); https://elemental.medium.com/the-science-of-shame-e1cb32f6f2a.

Advisory Board. "Charted: Physicians' Mental Health in 2023." *Advisory Board* (March 8, 2023); https://www.advisory.com/daily-briefing/2023/03/10/physician-suicide.

Ahlzen, R. "Suffering, Authenticity, and Physician-Assisted Suicide." *Medicine, Health Care and Philosophy* 23 (July 13, 2020): 353–59; doi:10.1007/s11019-019-09929-z.

Allphin, Claire. "An Unhealable Wound: Left by Suicide." *Journal of Analytical Psychology 63*, no. 5 (November 2018): 641–55; doi: 10.1111/1468-5922.12449.

American Journal of Play. "Playing on the Right Side of the Brain: An Interview with Allan N. Schore." *American Journal of Play 9*, no. 2 (Winter 2017): 105–42; https://www.museumofplay.org/app/uploads/2022/01/9-2-interview.pdf.

American Psychiatric Association. "What Is Post-Traumatic Stress Disorder (PTSD)?" *American Psychiatric Association* (November 2022); https://www.psychiatry.org/patients-families/ptsd/what-is-ptsd.

Asomatou, Arezina, Athanasios, Tselebis, Dionisios, Bratis, Kyriakos, Stavrianakos, Georgios, Zafeiropoulos, Argyro, Pachi, and Georgios, Moussas. "The Act of Suicide in Greek Mythology." *Encephalos* 53 (2016): 65–75; www.encephalos.gr/pdf/53-4-01e.pdf.

Auden, W. H. Quoted in *Goodreads* (n.d., accessed September 11, 2023); https://goodreads.com.

Balk, Gene. "Seattle Was the Saddest Metro Area in the Nation Last Month, Survey Shows." *Seattle Times* (December 17, 2020).

⸻. "Suicide Rate up in All Regions of Washington—but Why? 'No One Is Exactly Sure' Expert Says." *Seattle Times* (June 15, 2018).

Batt-Rawden, Samantha S., Margaret S. Chisolm, Blair Anton, and Tabor E. Flickinger. "Teaching Empathy to Medical Students: An Updated, Systematic Review." *Academic Medicine* 88, no. 8 (August 2013): 1171–77; doi: 10.1097/ACM.0b013e318299f3e3.

Best, Katherine. "Suicide: An Archetypal Perspective." *The Assisi Institute Journal* 1, no. 1, article 6 (2014); https://digitalcommons.providence.edu/assisi_journal/vol1/iss1/6.

Bible Tools. "Strong's #849: Autocheir." *BibleTools, Greek/Hebrew Definitions* (n.d., accessed August 21, 2023); https://www.bibletools.org/index.cfm?cx=006538976850733148404%3Aotqd4eea0gk&cof=FORID%3A9&ie=UTF-8&fuseaction=search.results&q=autocheir&sa=Search.

Blum, Karen. "Suicides Rise in Black Population During Covid-19 Pandemic." *Johns Hopkins Medicine* (April 20, 2021); https://

Bibliography

www.hopkinsmedicine.org/news/articles/2021/04/suicides-rise-in-black-population-during-covid-19-pandemic.

Bonner, Marla. Interview of Kendra Thorne in "Rurality's Relationship to Suicide Risk." APA Journals Dialogue Episode 24, *American Psychological Association* (2017); https://www.apa.org/pubs/highlights/podcasts/episode-24.

Bradvik, Louise. "Suicide Risk and Mental Disorders." *International Journal of Environmental Research and Public Health* 15, no. 9 (September 2018); https://www.mdpi.com/1660-4601/15/9/2028.

Branigin, Anne. "More Women than Ever Own Guns. Could That Change Gun Laws?" *Washington* Post (June 6, 2022); https://www.washingtonpost.com/nation/2022/06/06/women-gun-owners-changing-laws/.

Brehier, Emile. *The History of Philosophy: The Hellenic Age.* Chicago: University of Chicago Press, 1963.

Brittanica. "Anatta." *Brittanica* (n.d., accessed August 23, 2023); www.britannica.com/topic/soul-religion-and-philosophy.

Brown, Brené. *Atlas of the Heart: Mapping Meaningful Connection and the Language of Human Experience.* New York, NY: Random House, 2021.

Camus, Albert. *The Myth of Sisyphus.* Translated by Justin O'Brien. New York, NY: Vintage Books, 2018.

Chatterjee, Rhitu. "U.S. Suicide Rates Are Rising Faster among Women than Men." *NPR Morning Edition* (June 14, 2018); https://www.npr.org/sections/health-shots/2018/06/14/619338703/u-s-suicides-rates-are-rising-faster-among-women-than-men.

Cherry, Kendra. "Freud's Eros and Thanatos Theory: Life and Death Drives." *Verywell Mind*. Updated March 16, 2023; https://www.verywellmind.com/life-and-death-instincts-2795847.

Choices Psychotherapy. "Top 10 Jobs with Highest Suicide Rates." *Choices Psychotherapy* (September 15, 2022); https://choicespsychotherapy.net/jobs-with-highest-suicide-rates/.

Cholbi, Michael. "Suicide." *Stanford Encyclopedia of Philosophy*. Rev. November 9, 2021; https://plato.stanford.edu/entries/suicide/#AncClaVieSui.

Cicero. *De Officiis*, 3: 60–61. Quoted in the *Stanford Encyclopedia of Philosophy* (May 18, 2004, rev. November 9, 2021); https://plato.stanford.edu/entries/suicide/.

Clements-Nolle, Kristen, Matthew Wolden, and Jessey Bargmann-Losche. "Childhood Trauma and Risk for Past and Future Suicide Attempts among Women in Prison." *Women's Health Issues* 19, no. 3 (May–June 2000): 185–92.

Contreras, Antonieta. "Unveiling the Brain's Role in Modern Trauma Treatment: Unleashing Neuroscience's Potential for Lasting Recovery." *Medium* (September 15, 2020); https://contrerasantonieta.medium.com/the-science-of-trauma-treatment-2e5f25a7d82.

Cook, Katy. "What Is Shame and How Does It Show Up in Your Life and Work?" *Psychology Today* (February 11, 2021); https://www.psychologytoday.com/us/blog/emotional-intelligence/202102/what-is-shame-and-how-does-it-show-in-your-life-and-work#.

Bibliography

The Counselling Directory. "The Psychodynamics of Suicide." *Counselling Directory* (March 15, 2013); https://www.counselling-directory.org.uk/memberarticles/the-psychodynamics-of-suicide.

Crisis House. "What Is Trauma?" *Crisis House* (July 12, 2022); https:www.crisishouse.org/post/what-is-trauma.

Czeisler, Mark É., Rashon I. Lane, Emiko Petrosky, Joshua F. Wiley, Aleta Christensen, Rashid Njai, Matthew D. Weaver et al. "Mental Health, Substance Use, and Suicidal Ideation during the COVID-19 Pandemic—United States, June 24–30, 2020." *CDC Morbidity and Mortality Weekly Report* 69, no. 32 (August 14, 2020): 1049–57; https://www.cdc.gov/mmwr/volumes/69/wr/mm6932a1.htm.

Dastagir, Alia E. "More and More Americans Are Dying by Suicide. What Are We Missing?" *USA Today* (January 30, 2020); https://www.usatoday.com/story/news/nation/2020/01/30/u-s-suicide-rate-rose-again-2018-how-can-suicide-prevention-save-lives/4616479002/.

Dattani, Saloni, Lucas Rodés-Guirao, Hannah Ritchie, Max Roser, and Esteban Ortiz-Ospina.

"Suicides." *Our World in Data* (2023); https://ourworldindata.org/suicide?insight=suicide-deaths-are-more-common-among-men#key-insights-on-suicide.

Davis, Margaret T., Tracy Witte, and Frank Weathers. "Post-Traumatic Stress Disorder and Suicidal Ideation: The Role of Specific Symptoms within the Framework of the Interpersonal-Psychological Theory of Suicide."

Psychological Trauma, Theory, Research, Practice and Policy 6, no. 6 (October 14, 2013): 610–18.

DeYoung, Patricia A. *Understanding and Treating Chronic Shame: A Relational/Neurological Approach.* New York, NY: Routledge, 2015.

DSM-5: *Desk Reference to the Diagnostic Criteria* (Washington, DC: American Psychiatric Association, 2013).

Dwivedi, Yogesh, ed. *The Neurobiological Basis of Suicide.* Boca Raton, FL: CRC Press, Taylor and Francis Group, 2012.

Edelman, Sandra. *Turning the Gorgon: A Meditation on Shame.* Woodstock, CT: Spring Publications, 1998.

Edinger, Edward F. *Anatomy of the Psyche: Alchemical Symbolism in Psychotherapy.* LaSalle, IL: Open Court, 1985.

———. *Ego and Archetype.* Boulder: Shambala, 1972.

———. *Encounter with the Self: A Jungian Commentary on Willian Blake's Illustrations of the Book of Job.* Toronto: Inner City Books, 1986.

Estés, Clarissa Pinkola. *Women Who Run with the Wolves*: *Myths and Stories of the Wild Woman Archetype.* New York, NY: Ballantine Books, 1992.

Etymology Online Dictionary. "Euthanize." *Etymology Online Dictionary* (n.d., accessed August 21, 2023); https://www.etymonline.com/word/euthanize.

Everytown. "Gun Violence in America." *Everytown* (May 19, 2020); https://everytownresearch.org/report/gun-violence-in-america/.

Bibliography

_____. "The Rise of Firearm Suicide Among Young Americans." *Everytown* (June 2, 2022); https://everytownresearch.org/report/the-rise-of-firearm-suicide-among-young-americans/.

Fawcett, Jan. "Diagnosis, Traits, States, and Comorbidity in Suicide." In Dwivedi, *The Neurobiological Basis of Suicide*, ch. 1.

Field, Jena. See Abramson, Ashley.

Firestone, Lisa. "The Anti-Self vs. the True Self." *Psychalive*. Accessed August 5, 2023; https://www.psychalive.org/the-anti-self-vs-the-true-self/.

Fishkin, Gerald Loren. *The Science of Shame and Its Treatment*. Marion, MI: Parkhurst Brothers, 2016.

Freeman, Aislinné, Roland Mergl, Elisabeth Kohls, Andras Szekely, Ricardo Gusmao, Ella Arensman, Nicole Koburger, Ulrich Hegerl, Ulrich Hegerl, and Christine Rummel-Kluge. "A Cross-National Study on Gender Differences in Suicide Intent," *BMC Psychiatry* 17, n. 234 (June 29, 2017); bmcpsychiatry.biomedcentral.com/articles/10.1186/s12888-017-1398-8.

Gellert, Michael. *Legacy of Darkness and Light: Our Cultural Icons and Their God Complex*. Virginia Beach, VA: Koehlerbooks, 2023.

Gersch, Kaye. "Suicide and the Soul: A New Perspective." *Dr. Kaye Gersch, PhD* (March 22, 2021); https://www.kayegersch.com/suicide-and-soul.

Ghorayshi, Azeen and Roni Caryn Rabin. "Teen Girls Report Record Levels of Sadness, C.D.C. Finds." *New York Times*

(February 13, 2023); https://www.nytimes.com/2023/02/13/health/teen-girls-sadness-suicide-violence.html.

Global Economy. "Suicides—Country Rankings." *Global Economy*; https://www.theglobaleconomy.com/ramnkings/suicides/.

Goldblatt, Mark J. "The Psychodynamics of Hope in Suicidal Despair." *Scandinavian Psychoanalytic Review* 40, no. 1 (May 2, 2017): abstract; doi:10.1080/01062301.2017.1312 219.

Goldsmith, S. K., T. C. Pellmar, A. M. Kleinman, and W. E. Bunney, eds. *Reducing Suicide: A National Imperative*. Washington, DC: National Academies Press, 2002. Ch. 5, "Childhood Trauma as a Risk Factor for Suicidality." *NIH*; https://www.ncbi.nlm.nih.gov/books/NBK220932/.

Gramlich, John. "What the Data Says about Gun Deaths in the U.S." *Pew Research Center* (April 26, 2023); www.pewresearch.org/short-reads/2023/04/26/what-the-data-says-about-gun-deaths-in-the-u-s/.

Hallowell, Edward. "ADHD and Shame." *Dr. Hallowell* (April 26, 2017); https://drhallowell.com. 2017/04/26. adhd-and-shame.

Harding, Esther. *The Value and Meaning of Depression*. New York, NY: Analytical Psychology Club of New York, Inc., 1970.

Harkavy-Friedman, Jill. "Ask Dr. Jill: Does Mental Illness Play a Role in Suicide?" *American Foundation for Suicide Prevention* (February 7, 2020); https://afsp.org/story/ask-dr-jill-does-mental-illness-play-a-role-in-suicide/.

Bibliography

Hedegaard, Holly, Sally C. Curtin, and Margaret Warner. "Increase in Suicide Mortality in the U.S., 1999–2018." *Centers for Disease Control, NCHS Data Brief*, no. 362 (April 2020); https://www.cdc.gov/nchs/data/databriefs/db362-h.pdf.

Hendin, Herbert. "The Psychodynamics of Suicide." *International Review of Psychiatry* 4, no. 2 (1992): 157–67; doi: 3109/0954026920966313.

Hillman, James. *Revisioning Psychology*. New York, NY: Harper & Row, 1975. The Joyous Science.

———. Suicide and the Soul. 3rd, rev. ed. Thompson, CT: Spring Publications, 2020.

Hollis, James. *Swamplands of the Soul; New Life in Dismal Places*. Inner City Books. 1996. P.8 Sounds True podcast, June 9, 2020; resources.soundstrue.com/podcast/james-hollisthe-goal-of-life-is-meaning-not-happiness/.

———. *Living between Worlds; Finding Personal Resilience in Changing Times*. Boulder: Sounds True, 2020.

———. *Swamplands of the Soul: New Life in Dismal Places*. Toronto: Inner City Books, 1996.

Holloway, Henry. "Whale of Pain: The Heartbreaking Story of Killer Whale Named Hugo Who 'Killed Himself' by Repeatedly Ramming Head against Tank." *The Sun* (October 2, 2022); https://www.thesun.co.uk/news/16148622/hugo-killer-whale-orca-killed-himself/.

Inman, Cory S., Kelly R. Bijanki, David I. Bass, Robert E. Gross, Stephan Hamann, and Jon T. Willie. "Human Amygdala Stimulation Effects on Emotion Physiology and

Emotional Experience." *Neuropsychologia* 145 (August 2020); https:// www.sciencedirect.com/science/article/abs/pii/S002839321830112X?via%3Dihub.

Jacoby, Mario. *Shame and the Origins of Self-Esteem; A Jungian Approach*. New York, NY: Routledge, 2017.

Joiner, Thomas. *Why People Die by Suicide*. Cambridge, MA and London: Harvard University Press, 2005.

Joseph, Stephen. "What is Trauma? Is It Time to Dump the Diagnosis of PTSD?" *Psychology Today* (January 5, 2012); https://www.psychologytoday.com/us/blog/what-doesnt-kill-us/201201/what-is-trauma.

Jung, C. G. *Aion: Researches into the Phenomenology of the Self*. Vol. 9, pt. 2 of *The Collected Works of C. G. Jung*. 2nd ed. Edited by Sir Herbert Read, Michael Fordham, Gerhard Adler, and William McGuire. Translated by R. F. C. Hull. London and New York: Routledge, 2014.

_____. *Answer to Job*. Vol. 11 of *The Collected Works of C. G. Jung*. Translated by R. F. C. Hull. Princeton, NJ: Princeton University Press, 1954.

_____. *C. G. Jung Letters, Volume 1: 1906–1950*. Edited by Gerhard Adler and Aniela Jaffé. Translated by R. F. C. Hull. Princeton: Princeton University Press, 1973.

_____. *C. G. Jung Letters, Volume 2: 1951–1961*. Edited by Gerhard Adler and Aniela Jaffé. Translated by R. F. C. Hull. Princeton: Princeton University Press, 1976.

_____. *Man and His Symbols*. New York, NY: Dell Publishing, 1968.

———. *The Practice of Psychotherapy: Essays on the Psychology of the Transference and Other Subjects*. Vol. 16 of *The Collected Works of C.G. Jung*. Edited by Gerhard Adler. Translated by R. F. C. Hull. Princeton, NJ: Princeton University Press, 1954.

———. *Psychological Types*. Vol. 6 of *The Collected Works of C. G. Jung*. Edited by Gerhard Adler. Translated by R. F. C. Hull. Princeton, NJ: Princeton University Press, 1971.

———. *The Structure and Dynamics of the Psyche*. Vol. 8 of *The Collected Works of C.G. Jung*. 2nd ed. Edited by Gerhard Adler. Translated by R. F. C. Hull. Princeton, NJ: Princeton University Press, 1970.

———. *Symbols of Transformation*. Vol. 5 of *The Collected Works of C. G. Jung*. 2nd ed. Edited by Gerhard Adler. Translated by R. F. C. Hull. Princeton, NJ: Princeton University Press, 1956.

———. *Two Essays on Analytical Psychology*. Vol. 7 of *The Collected Works of C. G. Jung*. Edited by Gerhard Adler. Translated by R. F. C. Hull. Princeton, NJ: Princeton University Press 1953.

Kaieteur News. "Suicide rates Increased by 60 Percent Worldwide in Last 45 Years—WHO. *Kaieteur News* (September 11, 2111); https://www.kaieteurnewsonline.com/2011/09/11/suicide-rates-increased-by-60-percent-worldwide-in-last-45-years-who/.

Kalafat, John, and David Lester. "Shame and Suicide: A Case Study." *Death Studies* 24, no. 2 (March 2000): 157–62; https://doi.org/10.1080/074811800200621.

Kalmoe, Molly C., Matthew B. Chapman, Jessica A. Gold, and Andrea M. Giedinghagen. "Physician Suicide: A Call to Action." *Missouri Medicine* 116, no. 3 (May–June 2019): 211–16; https://www.ncbi.nlm.nih.gov/pmc/articles/PMC6690303/.

Kaplan, Kalman J. *Living a Purposeful Life: Searching for Meaning in All the Wrong Places*. Eugene, OR: Wipf & Stock, 2020.

Kaufman, Gershen. *Journal of Counseling Psychology*, 1974. Vol 21, No 6, p.1.

———, *The Psychology of Shame*. New York, NY: Springer, 1989.

Klopfer, Bruno. "Suicide: The Jungian Point of View." In *The Cry for Help*. Edited by Norman L. Farberow and Edwin S. Shneidman. New York, NY: McGraw-Hill, 1961.

Kulp, Maria, Nonia Williams Korteling, and Kathy McKay, eds. *Searching for Words: How Can We Tell Our Stories of Suicide*. Boston: Brill, 2013), 89–100; https:// brill.com/display/book/edcoll/9781848882195/BP000009.xml.

Leonard, Jayne. "What is Trauma? What to Know." *Medical News Today* (June 3, 2020); https//www.medicalnewstoday.com/articles/trauma.

Lester, David. "The Role of Shame in Suicide." *Suicide and Life-Threatening Behavior* 27, no. 4 (December 30, 2010); https://doi.org/10.1111/j.1943-278X.1997.tb00514.x.

Lewis, Michael. *Shame: The Exposed Self*. New York, NY: Free Press, 1992.

Lorenz, Hendrik. "Ancient Theories of Soul." *Stanford Encyclopedia of Philosophy*. Rev. April 22, 2009; https://plato.stanford.edu › entries › ancient-soul.

Bibliography

Magnier, Mark. "In Southern India, Relatives Sometimes Quietly Kill Their Elders." *Los Angeles Times* (January 15, 2013); https://www.latimes.com/world/la-xpm-2013-jan-15-la-fg-india-mercy-killings-20130116-story.html.

Maiese, Aniello, Lorenzo Gitto, Massimiliano dell'Aquila, and Giorgio Bolino. "A Peculiar Case of Suicide Enacted through the Ancient Japanese Ritual of *Jigai*." *American Journal of Forensic Medicine and Pathology* 35, no. 1 (March 2014):8–10; doi: 10.1097/PAF.0000000000000070.

Mann, Denise. "Pandemic Tied to Higher Suicide Rate in Blacks, Lowered Rate in Whites: Study." *HealthDay*, Dec 17, 2020; https://consumer.healthday.com/12-17-pandemic-is-raising-suicide-rate-for-blacks-lowering-it-for-whites-2649481957.html.

Marschall, Amy. "The Four Fear Responses: Fight, Flight, Freeze, and Fawn." *Verywell Mind*. Updated October 26, 2021; https://www.verywellmind.com/the-four-fear-responses-fight-flight-freeze-and-fawn-5205083.

Martin, Clancy. "Anthony Bourdain's Death Has Us Asking the Wrong Questions about Suicide." *Los Angeles Times* (October 11, 2022); https://www.latimes.com/opinion/story/2022-10-11/anthony-bourdain-book-suicide.

Matheson, John. "Physician Suicide." *American College of Emergency Physicians* (2023); https://www.acep.org/life-as-a-physician/wellness/wellness/wellness-week-articles/physician-suicide/.

Mathew, Soumya. "Thalaikoothal; Killing of the Already Withering." *Kaleidoscope* (April 13, 2016);

https://soumyamathew94.wordpress.com/2016/04/16/thalaikoothal-killing-of-the-already-withering/).

McCall, W. Vaughn, and Carmen G. Black. "The Link between Suicide and Insomnia: Theoretical Mechanisms." *Current Psychiatry Reports* 15, no. 9 (September 1, 2014); https://doi:10.1007/s11920-013-0389-9.

McGirr, A., J. Renaud, A. Bureau, M. Seguin, A. Lesage, and G. Turecki. "Impulsive-Aggressive Behaviors and Completed Suicide across the Life Cycle: A Predisposition for Younger Age of Suicide." *Cambridge University Press*, September 6, 2007; https://www.cambridge.org/core/journals/psychological-medicine/article/abs/impulsiveaggressive-behaviours-and-completed-suicide-across-the-life-cycle-a-predisposition-for-younger-age-of-suicide/.

McKeown, R. E., Steven P. Cuffe, and Richard M. Schulz. "US Suicide Rates by Age Group, 1970–2002: An Examination of Recent Trends." *American Journal of Public Health* 96, no. 10 (October 1, 2006): 1744–51; doi:10.2105/AJPH. 066951.

Mcleod, Saul. "Erik Erikson's Stages of Psychosocial Development." *Simply Psychology* (2013). Updated August 2, 2023; https://www.simplypsychology.org/erik-erikson.html.

Mental Health Daily. "Top 11 Professions with Highest Suicide Rates," *Mental Health Daily* (January 6, 2015); https://mentalhealthdaily.com/2015/01/06/top-11-professions-with-highest-suicide-rates/.

Mereish, Ethan H., Jessica R. Peters, and Shirley Yen. "Minority Stress and Relational Mechanisms of Suicide among Sexual

Bibliography

Minorities: Subgroup Differences in the Associations between Heterosexist Victimization, Shame, Rejection Sensitivity, and Suicide Risk." *National Library of Medicine* (March 31, 2018); https:// pubmed.ncbi.nlm.nih.gov/29604113/.

Middleton, Paul. "The 'Noble Death' of Judas Iscariot: A Reconsideration of Suicide in the Bible and Early Christianity." *Journal of Religion and Violence* 6 no. 2 (2018): abstract; https:// www.jstor.org/stable/26671573.

Miezio, Adam. "Know the 7 types of Trauma Like a Psychotherapist." *Psychedelic Support* (May 3, 2022). Updated March 6, 2023; https://psychedelic.support/resources/know-the-7-types-of-trauma-like-a-psychotherapist/.

Mikhailova, Olga. "Suicide in Psychoanalysis." *Psychoanalytic Social Work* 12, no. 2 (2006): 19–45; doi: 10.1300/J032v12n02_02.

Mind. "Post-Traumatic Stress Disorder." *Mind* (January 2021); https://www.mind.org.uk/media/7135/ptsd-and-complex-ptsd-2021-pdf-version.pdf.

Missouri University School of Medicine. "What Is Euthanasia?" *Missouri University School of Medicine, Center for Health Ethics* (2023); https://medicine.missouri.edu/centers-institutes-labs/health-ethics/faq/euthanasia.

Montgomery County Emergency Service. "Trauma and Suicide Risk." *MCES*. Accessed September 1, 2023; https:// mces.org/WordPress/wp-content/uploads/2021/12/TraumaandRisk.pdf.

Mueller, Anna S., Seth Abrutyn, Bernice Pescosolido, and Sarah Diefendorf. "The Social Roots of Suicide: Theorizing

How the External Social World Matters to Suicide and Suicide Prevention." *Frontiers in Psychology* 12 (March 31, 2021); https:// www.frontiersin.org/articles/10.3389/fpsyg.2021.621569/full.

National Institute of Mental Health. "Suicide Is a Leading Cause of Death in the United States." *National Institute of Mental Health* (n.d., accessed November 8, 2023); https://www.nimh.nih.gov/health/statistics/suicide.

Nestadt, Paul Sasha. Quoted in University of Rochester Medical Center. "Pandemic Tied to Higher Suicide Rate in Blacks, Lowered Rate in Whites: Study." *University of Rochester Medical Center* (December 17, 2020); www.urmc.rochester.edu/encyclopedia/content.aspx?contenttypeid=6&contentid=1649481957.

Nietzsche, Frederich. *Quoted in Goodreads* (n.d., accessed August 29, 2023); https://www.goodreads.com. The Joyous Science. Based on the book by Friedrich Nietzsche. 1882. Die frohliche Wissenschaft

Nora, Pierre. "Memory and History: Les Lieux de Mémoire." *Representations* 26 (Spring 1989): 7–24; https://is.muni.cz/el/1423/podzim2017/SOC571/Nora_105.pdf.

Olivine, Ashley. "What is Trauma? Types, Stages, and Treatment." *Verywell Health* (January 4, 2022); https://www.verywellhealth.com/what-is-trauma-5212104.

Oxford Reference. "Euthanasia." *Oxford Reference* (n.d., accessed August 21, 2023);

www.oxfordreference.com/display/10.1093/acref/ 9780198609810.001.0001/acref-9780198609810-e-2515;jsessionid=5E145487A816F826D5B6E7BE59E7556A.

Parker, Kim, Juliana Menasce Horowitz, Ruth Igielnik, J. Baxter Oliphant, and Anna Brown. "The Demographics of Gun Ownership." *Pew Research Center* (June 22, 2017); https://www.pewresearch.org/social-trends/2017/06/22/the-demographics-of-gun-ownership/.

Paturel, Amy. "Healing the Very Youngest Healers." *AAMC* (January 21, 2020); https://www.aamc.org/news/healing-very-youngest-healers.

Peterson, Cora, Aaron Sussell, Jia Li, Pamela K. Schumacher, Kristin Yeoman, and Deborah M. Stone. "Suicide Rates by Industry and Occupation—National Violent Death Reporting System, 32 States, 2016." *CDC Weekly* 69, no. 3 (January 24, 2020): 57–62; https://www.cdc.gov/mmwr/volumes/69/wr/mm6903a1.htm.

Pigeon, Wilfred R., Peter C. Britton, Mark A. Ilgen, Ben Chapman, and Kenneth R. Conner. "Sleep Disturbance Preceding Suicide Among Veterans." *American Journal of Public Health* 102, suppl. 1 (March 2012): S93–S97; https://ajph.aphapublications.org/doi/10.2105/AJPH.2011.300470.

Piretti, Lucra, Edoardo Pappaianni, Alberta Lunardelli, Irene Zorzenon, Maja Ukmar, Valentina Pesavento, Raffaella Ida Rumiati et al. "The Role of Amygdala in Self-Conscious Emotions in a Patient with Acquired Bilateral Damage." *Frontiers in Neuroscience* 14 (July 8, 2020); https://doi.org/10.3389/fnins.2020.00677.

Piscopo, Kathryn, Rachel N. Lipari, Jennifer Cooney, and Cristie Glasheen. "Suicidal Thoughts and Behavior among Adults: Results from the 2015 National Survey on Drug Use and Health." *SAMHSA: NSDUH Data Review* (September 2016); www.samhsa.gov/data/sites/default/files/NSDUH-DR-FFR3-2015/NSDUH-DR-FFR3-2015.pdf.

Plutchik, Robert, and Herman M. van Praag. "Psychosocial Correlates of Suicide and Violence Risk." In *Violence and Suicidality: Perspectives in Clinical and Psychobiological Research; Clinical and Experimental Psychiatry.* Edited by Herman M. Van Praag, Robert Plutchik, and Alan Apter, 37–65. Levittown, PA: Brunner/Mazel, 1990.

Pompili, Maurizio, Marco Innamorati, Michele Raja, Ilaria Falcone, Giuseppe Ducci, Gloria Angeletti, David Lester et al. "Suicide Risk in Depression and Bipolar Disorder: Do Impulsiveness-Aggressiveness and Pharmacotherapy Predict Suicidal Intent?" *Neuropsychiatric Disease and Treatment* 4, no.1 (February 1, 2008): 247–255; doi: 10.2147/ndt.s2192.

Pridmore, Saxby, Jamshid Ahmadi, and William Pridmore. "Two Mistaken Beliefs about Suicide." *Iran Journal of Psychiatry* 14, no. 2 (April 2019): 182–83.

Psych Central. "Freud's Theory of Depression and Guilt." *Psych Central.* Updated March 30, 2022; http:/ psychcentral.com/depression/was-freud-right-about-depression-and-guilt.

Puchko, Kristy. "15 Eerie Things about Japan's Suicide Forest." *Mental Floss* (January 8, 2016, updated June 7, 2023); https://www.mentalfloss.com/article/73288/15-eerie-things-about-japans-suicide-forest.

Bibliography

Pulcu, Erdem, Karen Lythe, Rebecca Elliott, Sophie Green, Jorge Moll, John F. W. Deakin, and Roland Zahn. "Increased Amygdala Response to Shame in Remitted Major Depressive Disorder." *PLoSONE 9*, no. 1 (2014); https://doi.org/10.1371/journal.pone.0086900.

Purrington, Mr. "Carl Jung's Views on Suicide—Quotations." *Carl Jung Depth Psychology* (May 11, 2020); https://carljungdepthpsychologysite.blog/2020/05/11/carl-jungs-views-on-suicide/.

Rabin, Roni Caryn. "U.S. Suicides Declined Overall in 2020 but May Have Risen among People of Color," *New York Times* (April 15, 2021); https:// www.nytimes.com/2021/04/15/health/coronavirus-suicide-cdc.html.

Raphling, D. L. "Dreams and Suicide Attempts." *Journal of Nervous and Mental Disease* 151, no. 6 (December 1970): 404–10.

Richards, Joscelyn. "Cohabitation and the Negative Therapeutic Reaction." *Journal of Psychoanalytic Psychotherapy* 7, no. 3 (1993): 223–39.

Rosen, David. *Transforming Depression: Healing the Soul through Creativity*. Wellington, FL: Nicolas-Hays, 1993.

Roarty, Sinead. "Death Wishing and Cultural Memory: A Walk through Japan's 'Suicide Forest.'" In Maria Kulp, Nonia Williams Korteling, and Kathy McKay, eds. *Searching for Words: How Can We Tell Our Stories of Suicide*, 89–100. Boston: Brill, 2013; https://brill.com/display/book/edcoll/9781848882195/BP000009.xml.

Samarasekera, Dujeepa D., Shuh Shing Lee, Su Ping Yeo, and Gominda Ponnamperuma. "Development of Student Empathy during Medical Education: Changes and the Influence of Context and Training." *Korean Journal of Medical Education* 34, no. 1 (March 2022): 17–26; doi: 10.3946/kjme.2022.216.

Schumacher, Helene. "Why More Men than Women Die by Suicide." *BBC Future* (March 17, 2019); https://www.bbc.com›future›article›20190313-why-more-men-kill-themselves-than-women.

Seneca. "On the Proper Time to Slip the Cable." Letter 70. *The Ethics of Suicide Digital Archive* (accessed October 27, 2023); https://ethicsofsuicide.lib.utah.edu/selections/seneca/.

Sharp, Daryl. *Jungian Lexicon: A Primer of Terms and Concepts* (accessed November 3, 2023); www.psychceu.com/Jung/sharplexicon.html.

Sheats, Kameron J., Rebecca F. Wilson, Bridget H. Lyons, Shane P. D. Jack, Carter J. Betz, and Katherine A. Fowler. "Surveillance for Violent Deaths—National Violent Death Reporting System, 39 States, the District of Columbia, and Puerto Rico, 2018." *CDC Morbidity and Mortality Weekly Report* 71, no. 3 (January 28, 2022): 1–44; https://www.cdc.gov/mmwr/volumes/71/ss/ss7103a1.htm.

Shneidman, Edwin S. *The Suicidal Mind*. New York, NY: Oxford University Press, 1996.

Sinason, Michael. "Who Is the Mad Voice Inside?" *Psychoanalytic Psychotherapy* 7, no. 3 (1993): 207–21.

Bibliography

Slaby, Andrew Edmund. "Creativity, Depression and Suicide." *Wiley Online Library* (Summer 1992); https://doi.org/10.1111/j.1943-278X.1992.tb00226.x.

Statista. "Gun ownership in the U.S. 1972–2022." *Statista* (June 2, 2023); https://www.statista.com/statistics/249740/percentage-of-households-in-the-united-states-owning-a-firearm/.

Stone, Deborah M., Christopher M. Jones, and Karin A. Mack. "Changes in Suicide Rates—United States, 2018–2019." *CDC Morbidity and Mortality Weekly Report* 70, no. 8 (February 26, 2021): 261–68; https://www.cdc.gov/mmwr/volumes/70/wr/pdfs/mm7008a1-H.pdf.

Suicide Prevention Resource Center. "Scope of the Problem." *Suicide Prevention Resource Center*. Accessed September 13, 2023; https://www.sprc.org › about-suicide › scope.

Sulaiman, Amir. "You Will Be Somebody's Ancestor. Act Accordingly." On the album *You Will Be Somebody's Ancestor. Act Accordingly*. Spoken Word (2022); https://www.youtube.com/watch?v=pfTTRsaYSDU.

Szasz, T. "Suicide as a Moral Issue." The Freeman, 49:41-42 (July), 1999. Reproduced here by permission of Sheldon Richmond, Editor, Ideas on Liberty (formerly the Freeman). Ideas on Liberty is published by the Foundation for Economic Education, Irvington-on-Hudson, NY 10533.

Or original entry:

Szasz, Thomas S. "Suicide as a Moral Issue: Who Should Control When and How We Die?" *Foundation for Economic*

Education (July 1, 1999); https://fee.org/articles/suicide-as-a-moral-issue/.

Tanasugarn, Annie. "Spotting the Triggers in Covert Narcissism." *The Good Men Project* (January 20, 2021); https://goodmenproject.com/featured-content/spotting-the-triggers-in-covert-narcissism/.

Tangney, J.P. (1995). Recent Advances in the Empirical Study of Shame and Guilt. *American Behavioral Scientist*, 36(8), 1132-1145.

Taylor-Jones, Christi. "A Mother's Death, A Daughter's Birth." *Psychological Perspectives* 55, no. 3 (July 2012).

————. "When Shame Becomes Deadly: The Relationship between Suicidality and Shame; A Personal Perspective. *Psychological Perspectives* 66, no. 2 (2023).

Thatcher, Todd. "Can Emotional Trauma Cause Brain Damage?" *Highland Springs Clinic* (February 4, 2019); https://highlandspringsclinic.org/can-emotional-trauma-cause-brain-damage/.

Thomas, Naomi. "These Jobs Have Highest Suicide Rates in the United States, According to the CDC." *CNN Health* (November 15, 2018);

https://edition.cnn.com/2018/11/15/health/occupational-suicide-rate-cdc-study/index.html.

Thorne, K., Elizabeth Catherine Conti, Amy Fiske, and Joseph R. Scotti. "Traumatic Stress and Suicide Risk: The Role of Rural Origin." *Journal of Rural Mental Health 41*, n. 1 (2017): 42–53. http://dx.doi.org/10.1037/rmh0000062.

Bibliography

Tomkins, SS. *Affect, Imagery and Consciousness.* Vol. 2, p.118. New York: Springer & Co., 1963.

Tompkins Institute. "Nine Affects, Present at Birth, Combine with Life Experience to Form Emotion and Personality." *Tompkins Institute.* Accessed July 26, 2023; www.tomkins.org/what-tomkins-said/introduction.

_____, Price, E., Fiske, A., and Scotti, J. R. "Traumatic Stress and Suicide Risk: The Role of Rural Origin." *Journal of Rural Mental Health 41*, n. 1 (2017): 42–53; http://dx.doi.org/10.1037/rmh0000062.

Tick, Edward. *War and the Soul: Healing Our Nation's Veterans from Post-traumatic Stress Disorder.* Wheaton, IL: Quest Books, 2005.

Troya, M. Isabela, Matthew J. Spittal, Rosina Pendrous, Grace Crowley, Hayley C. Gorton, Kirsten Russell, Sadhbh Byrne et al. "Suicide Rates among Individuals from Ethic Minority Backgrounds: A Systematic Review and Meta-Analysis." *eClinicalMedicine/Lancet* 47, no. 101399 (May 2022); https://www.thelancet.com/journals/eclinm/article/PIIS2589-5370(22)00129-8/fulltext.

United Nations. "800,000 People Commit Suicide Each Year—WHO." *United Nations: UN News*, September 9, 2018; https://news.un.org/en/story/2018/09/1018761.

University of Rochester Medical Center. "Pandemic Tied to Higher Suicide Rate in Blacks, Lowered Rate in Whites: Study." *University of Rochester Medical Center* (December 17, 2020); www.urmc.rochester.edu/encyclopedia/content.aspx?contenttypeid=6&contentid=1649481957.

University of Washington. "Suicide More Prevalent than Homicide in US, but Most Americans Don't Know It." *UW News* (October 30, 2018); https://www.washington.edu/news/2018/10/30/suicide.

Unyte. "What Is Trauma?" *Unyte: Integrated Listening Systems* (September 13, 2018); https://integratedlistening.com/blog/what-is-trauma/.

UW Medicine. "State Data Reveal Fentanyl's Fatal Role across Age Groups." *UW Medicine/Newsroom* (December 8, 2021); https://newsroom.uw.edu/news/state-data-reveal-fentanyls-fatal-role-across-age-groups.

Van der Kolk, Bessel. *The Body Keeps the Score: Mind, Brain and Body in the Transformation of Trauma*. New York, NY: Penguin, 2015.

Ventriglio, Antonio, Cameron Watson, and Dinesh Bhugra. "Suicide among Doctors: A Narrative Review." *Indian Journal of Psychiatry* 62, no. 2 (March–April 2020): 114–120; doi: 10.4103/psychiatry.IndianJPsychiatry_767_19.

Wheelwright, Jane Hollister. *The Death of a Woman: How a Life Became Complete*. New York, NY: St. Martin's Press, 1981.

Wikipedia. "List of Countries by Suicide Rate" (WHO statistics). *Wikipedia* (updated August 5, 2023); https://en.wikipedia.org/wiki/List_of_countries_by_suicide_rate.

_____. "Philosophy of Suicide." *Wikipedia* (last updated August 14, 2023); https://en.wikipedia.org/wiki/Philosophy_of_suicide.

Bibliography

———. "Senicide." *Wikipedia* (last updated August 14, 2023); https://en.wikipedia.org/wiki/Senicide.

———. "Suicide in Antiquity." *Wikipedia* (last updated August 11, 2023); en.wikipedia.org/wiki/Suicide_in_antiquity.

Wiley Online Library. "Do Stock Market Fluctuations Affect Suicide Rates?" *Wiley Online Library* (July 27, 2020); https://onlinelibrary.wiley.com/doi/full/10.1111/jfir.12224.

Wille, Robbert. "The Shame of Existing: An Extreme Form of Shame." *International Journal of Psychoanalysis* 95, no. 4 (August 2014); https://pubmed.ncbi.nlm.nih.gov/24916725/

Winborn, Mark. "James Hillman on Soul." *The Psychoanalytic Muse* (August 19, 2011): https://psychoanalyticmuse.blogspot.com/2011/08/james-hillman-on-soul.html.

Winfrey, Oprah. Interviews of Brené Brown. Two-part series on "Super Soul Sunday" (March 17 and 24, 2013); www.oprah.com/search.html?q=Brene+Brown.

Wisdom Library. "Ātmāhuti," *Wisdom Library* (last updated October 25, 2021); www.wisdomlib.org/definition/atmahuti.

Wisniewski, Tomasz Piotr, Brendan John Lambe, and Keshab Shrestha. December 2020. "Do Stock Market Fluctuations Affect Suicide Rates?" *Journal of Financial Research, Southern Finance Association: Southwestern Finance Association*, vol. 43(4), p. 737-765.

Woodman, Marion. *The Pregnant Virgin: A Process of Psychological Transformation*. Toronto: Inner City Books, 1985.

World Population Review. "Best Countries to Live in 2023." *World Population Review*. Accessed September 12, 2023);

https://worldpopulationreview.com/country-rankings/best-countries-to-live-in.

————. "Suicide Rate by Country, 2023." *World Population Review*. Accessed September 12, 2023; https://worldpopulationreview.com/country-rankings/suicide-rate-by-country.

Yoon, L. "Suicide in South Korea—Statistics & Facts." *Statista* (November 23, 2022); htttps://www.statista.com.

Young, Robert M. "Across the Borderline," *Psychoanalysis and Therapy: Robert M. Young Online Writings* (n.d., accessed September 11, 2023), 3–4; http://www.psychoanalysis-and-therapy.com. Keynote address to the Second International Conference on "Psychosis: Treatment of Choice?'" University of Essex, Colchester, September 23–15, 1994.

About the Author

Christi Taylor-Jones, MA, LMFT is a certified Jungian Analyst and writer, who is a frequent contributor to the journal *Psychological Perspectives* and other publications over the last thirty years. Her first book was *Midlife Parenting; A Guide to Having and Raising Kids in your 30s, 40s and Beyond.* She has also written and presented extensively on the issue of shame, depression and suicide.

Made in the USA
Las Vegas, NV
04 November 2024